The
WHISKY
KITCHEN

100 WAYS WITH WHISKY AND FOOD

**SHEILA McCONACHIE
& GRAHAM HARVEY**

Spirit of Speyside Chef of the Year

Acknowledgments

This book would not have been possible without the unconditional assistance and inspiration of some very special people. Our heartfelt thanks go to Ghillie Başan for believing we could do it; Graeme Wallace for his enthusiastic support; his designer for creating such a beautiful book and Sue Lawrence and Gavin Hewitt for their kind words. Our fantastic kitchen brigade: Kate, Paul, Cordula and Sam, for their amazing good humour and patience in the face of endless experiments. Special thanks go to Kate for her invaluable recipe-testing and to Marian for her ever willing recipe-tasting. Finally our love and thanks go to Rachel, Jennifer, Jamie and Gordon for their unfailing support and encouragement.

For Jack and Ada

Text © Sheila McConachie & Graham Harvey
Photography © Graeme Wallace

First published in Great Britain 2008 Revised 2008 Reprinted 2011

The rights of Sheila McConachie, Graham Harvey and Graeme Wallace to be identified as the authors and photographer of this work have been asserted by them in accordance with the Copyright, Designs and Patents Act 1988

Design – Kevin Jeffery
Printing – Printer Trento, Italy

Published by
GW Publishing
PO Box 6091
Thatcham
Berks
RG19 8XZ.

Tel + 44 (0)1635 268080
www.gwpublishing.com
www.whiskykitchen.com

ISBN 978-0-9554145-7-2

Contents

138 Highland Region

Accompaniments & Sauces

Contents

Foreword

I first met Graham Harvey at the Spirit of Speyside Chef of the Year competition in 2007 and was blown away by both his haggis veloute starter and his dessert of chocolate truffle torte. Our second encounter was in London where he had to recreate the dishes he had cooked for only 3 judges for a large room of discerning gourmets. His food was equally memorable.

For Graham and partner Sheila then to be asked to do a whisky cookbook makes enormous sense, for not only are they both brilliant technicians in the kitchen, Graham also knows a thing or two about whisky!

Look at the list of recipes: Lochnagar Chanterelles, Auchentoshan Stroganoff (try saying that after more than one dram!), Glenfiddich Raisin Bread….. these and the many others testify to the creativity of the cook and the expertise of the whisky connoisseur.

This is not a book full of twee dishes all too often found in so-called traditional Scottish restaurants that believe adding the words "whisky-drenched" to any ingredient from Aberdeen Angus beef to Highland venison makes it pleasing to the palate. In this book are recipes that combine both the food and whisky elements perfectly and make sense within the realms of both the kitchen and the distillery. They are also not too "cheffy" and are therefore do-able by most cooks whatever their standard. Best of all, however, they are delicious!

Sue Lawrence,
Author and President of The Guild of Food Writers

the WHISKY KITCHEN

Scotland is blessed with some of the finest produce in the world: seafood; shellfish; vegetables; soft fruits; meat and game, not to mention whisky - *uisge beatha - the water of life*. What better way to celebrate this than to marry whisky and food.

All the great culinary nations have long combined their wines, brandies and other spirits with their food but we have not had this tradition with our whisky, which is strange because Scotch whiskies enjoy such a variety of flavours and subtleties of taste that they cry out to be used in any kitchen of the world. They tenderise and cure meat and fish and they add a delicious often delicate quality to everything from meat, vegetables and fish to cakes and desserts. Wait till you try them with chocolate.....

In this collection of recipes combining whisky and food you will find hearty soups synonymous with the Scottish kitchen; beef, lamb and game in sumptuous dishes plus fish and shellfish creations that combine the flavours of the food and the particular nuances of the selected whisky. The recipes have been designed in such a way that 50ml whisky miniatures can be used to complete the dishes, but please do not let that stop you buying a full sized bottle of Scottish malt whisky when you find one you particularly enjoy.

The book also contains 4 section breaks based upon the recognised scotch whisky regions, here we have tried to give you a taste of the geography, produce and of course the whiskies of the Speyside, Highland, Lowland and the Islay and Islands regions. Having painted such an interesting picture of Scotland, both regionally and as a whole, we hope that you will come and experience it for yourself.

If you are looking for ideas for a dinner party, why not try the Velouté of Haggis laced with Glenfarclas, for your starter, it is such a simple recipe yet will thrill your guests. For the main course you could serve the Roast Salmon with Aberlour and Orange Jus and your guests will be amazed. Then for your finale, your chocoholic friends will just love the Glen Moray Chocolate Truffle Torte.

The marriage of food and wine or beer is a concept which promotes much animated discussion at the dinner table, matching whisky and food is no exception. The first step when matching whisky to a particular dish is to create an imaginary bridge between the food and the whisky, the purpose of this bridge is to link the two harmoniously by means of complementing or contrasting. The creation of this book has been a labour of love and our knowledge of the sometimes subtle, sometimes striking differences in the range of whiskies available has grown tremendously as a result. We hope that you will enjoy the fruits of our research as much as we have.

Once you start your own journey cooking with whisky we encourage you to experiment further, to go forth and invent your own recipes. To this end we have provided a whisky and food matching guide at the end of the book, just remember these are not hard and fast rules, they are guidelines from which to build your own repertoire of fantastic recipes.

For our own part we hope that you will enjoy discovering, perhaps re-discovering, the incredible range of malt whiskies available and the sometimes astonishing food combinations that are possible in the whisky kitchen.

sláinte and bon appetit
Sheila and Graham

Matching Whisky and Food

Creating a recipe begins with understanding the relationship between all of the ingredients and how they will work together to produce the final dish. Matching whisky and food is merely an extension of this process. Do you want to capture the nose, the background flavours or the finish? Is it your intention for the dish to taste of the chosen whisky, or are you trying to create a subtle layer of flavour that changes what you are cooking from a very good dish to one that is utterly sublime? So, to start, stick your nose in the glass and sniff. With each whisky you will find a host of different aromas, peat, wood-smoke, tea, dried fruits, sea air, liquorice, vanilla, toffee, honey, almonds, citrus – the list goes on and on.

Some whiskies can give you a hint as to how they would prefer to be used. Take a nose of Springbank 10 year old and it will cry out to be used in your next Christmas cake. Have a whiff of Glen Moray 16 year old and it will be telling you to get the chocolate out. Do you enjoy the sweeter notes found in Speyside malts or the heathery background so often present in Highland whisky? The citrus notes of Aberlour want to be matched with a delicate, oily fish like salmon. If you taste the whisky it might give you a few more clues. Cragganmore is an extremely complex whisky which is very versatile and works so well with a range of foods, look at our Scotch Onion Soup, Roast Belly Pork and Rhubarb Queen of Puddings. The unmistakeable peppery background of Talisker is a great seasoning for many a dish. I swear that Royal Lochnagar smells of woodland mushrooms and that is why it works so well with chanterelles and ceps. Like wine it takes time to get to know the complexities and individual personalities of all the different whiskies, but what a wonderful journey of discovery. Have fun!

As you will have seen from our recipes, whisky also makes a great marinade. Create a basic marinade by adding olive or hazelnut oil to your chosen whisky, lemon or lime juice and herbs for fish, vegetables or other light dishes. Add Worcestershire Sauce and thyme to add strength and depth of flavour for beef; orange juice and spices for duck; basil for Mediterranean vegetables and so on. Just remember not to marinate fish or beef for longer than 30 minutes and you can go ahead and make your own delicious marinades.

The following table marries food and whisky pairings that we know work and provides you with the opportunity to experiment for yourself. The guide is not a series of hard and fast rules, rather it is a starting point for your own series of wonderful creations. If your preference is for a particular type or regional style of whisky, look for the key notes of the whisky that you want to be evident in the dish, use the whisky sparingly at first and build up the recipe to one which captures what you are trying to achieve. You will probably find that the flavour of the whisky changes subtly during the cooking process, make notes of what happens and use these to increase your experience of matching whisky and food.

You may notice that we have a few clear favourite whiskies that we find particularly adaptable. Just as there can be endless debate about which Scotch is the best to drink, so there similar scope for further discussions about which whisky goes best with certain dishes. If we can in any small way be held responsible for fuelling the passions of those involved in this debate, we will be very pleased indeed.

Food Type	Ingredient	Style of Dish	Whisky Matches
shellfish	crab and lobster	soups	Caol Ila, Tomatin
		thermidore	Glenfarclas
		cold with salad	Glenfarclas
	crayfish	barbecued	Royal Lochnagar, Talisker
		spicy	Glenfarclas
	mussels, clams, whelks and other bivalves	garlicky, herby dishes like marinière	Bunnahabhain, Talisker
		in tarts and quiches	Hazelburn
		in shellfish soup	Caol Ila, Springbank
	prawns	spicy whisky lovers	Laphroaig – for the peaty
		spicy	Talisker, Arran
		creamy	Ardbeg, Talisker,
		cold with salad	a little Glenkinchie in the dressing
	scallops	pan seared	make a little creamy dressing with Tullibardine
		in risotto	Royal Lochnagar, Talisker
fish	delicate white fish	with creamy sauce	Ardbeg, Cragganmore
	firm white fish	with accompanying sauce	Hazelburn
		smoked	Talisker
	mackerel and other oily sea fish	smoked	BenRiach Dark Rum Wood Aberfeldy
		cold in salad	Tomintoul
	salmon	pan seared	Aberlour
		poached	Aberlour
		roast	Glengoyne
		smoked	Talisker, Aberlour or for peaty whisky lovers Laphroaig
		cured	Talisker, Aberlour
		cold in salad	A little Talisker in the dressing
meat	beef	roasted	Cragganmore, Auchentoshen
		prime steak cuts	Auchentoshen, Hazelburn, Highland Park
		burgers	Jura
		casseroled	Black Bottle, Cragganmore
	lamb	roasted	Jura, Cragganmore
		grilled chops	Jura
	pork	roasted	Royal Lochnagar, Cragganmore
		belly pork	Cragganmore
		pork fillet	Royal Lochnagar, Jura
		bacon and ham	Oban
game	guinea fowl	roast supremes	Cragganmore, Royal Lochnagar
	grouse	whole bird roasted	Tomintoul, Cragganmore
	pheasant, partridge or pigeon	roasted	Royal Lochnagar

Food Type	Ingredient	Style of Dish	Whisky Matches
	venison	seared breast	Royal Lochnagar
		roasted	Benromach
		prime steak cuts	Cragganmore
		casseroled	Jura, Cragganmore
poultry	chicken	roasted	Tullibardine
		seared or barbecued breast and thigh portions	Royal Lochnagar
		cold in salad	A little Cragganmore in the dressing
		soups	Old Pulteney
	duck	pan seared breast	Jura
		confit	Jura
		smoked	Jura
offal	haggis	any way is great	Glenfarclas
	liver	pâté	Glenfiddich, Glenfarclas
		fried or braised	Glenfarclas, Talisker
vegetables, pulses and fungi	fennel	braised	Hazelburn
	lentils, beans etc	casseroled	Auchentoshen, Aberfeldy
	mushrooms, cultivated	sauces and soups	Glenlivet
		cold salads	Auchentoshen, Glenfarclas
	mushrooms, wild	sauces and soups	Cragganmore, Royal Lochnagar
	onions	soup	Cragganmore
		marmalade	Aberlour a'bunadh
	potatoes	soups	Glenkinchie
	root	roasted	Hazelburn
pasta	any	with cheese based sauce	The Macallan
baking	biscuits	any	Teacher's, Balvenie
	fruit cakes		Benriach, Springbank
	soda bread		Glenkinchie
	steamed puddings		Benriach, Longmorn
fruits	baked	any	Glayva
	cherries	any	Aberlour
	figs	baked or grilled	Edradour
	mixed fruits	pan roasted	Glayva
	rhubarb	any	Cragganmore, Aberfeldy
	soft summer fruits	jams, chutney and jellies	Glen Moray, Cragganmore, Aberlour
desserts	brulée		Drambuie, Aberlour
	chocolate	any	The Macallan, Benriach, Drambuie, Glen Moray, Dalwhinnie, Arran
		with nuts	Auchentoshen, Tullibardine, Royal Lochnagar
dairy	blue cheese	cheeseboard, sauces, grilled	Edradour, Old Pulteney, The Macallan, Glenmorangie
	goat's cheese	grilled	Famous Grouse, Cragganmore

Scotch Vichyssoise

Glenkinchie 10 year old's distinctive floral notes and clean taste on the palate make for an excellent combination with this thick, creamy, chilled soup and works equally well when the soup is served hot.
This delightful soup is based on the very famous French potato and leek soup which is served cold, we have made it our own by adding the whisky.

Serves 8

▪ Begin by peeling and slicing the potatoes and chopping the celery finely. You can save time and energy by using a food processor for this task. Set aside while you prepare the leeks and onion.

▪ Cut the leeks lengthwise and wash them thoroughly because there can be quite a lot of dirt in between the leaves. Cut off the dark green parts and keep them for making stock or broth then slice the white parts thinly and chop the onion finely.

▪ Melt the butter and oil in a large saucepan and sweat the onion and leek gently for about 5 minutes until softened. It is very important not to let them brown. Then add the vegetables, stock, bay leaf, salt and pepper to the saucepan and bring to the boil, reduce the heat and allow to simmer for about 30 minutes or until the vegetables are very soft.

▪ Remove the bay leaf and pour the soup into a liquidiser or food processor and blend until very smooth. You will have to do this in batches. To make it even smoother, pass it through a fine sieve. Return the soup to a clean pan, season carefully to taste and stir in the whisky and cream. Now set the soup over ice to cool. Place in the fridge to chill down completely. This is a fairly thick soup but if becomes too thick, you can let it down with a little stock.

4 medium potatoes
1 stick of celery
4 large leeks,
1 small onion
*50g butter and a little olive oil
for frying*
*1.25 litres chicken stock (or use
vegetable stock for a delicious
veggie option)*
1 large bay leaf
*salt and freshly ground black pepper
to season*
225mls double cream
*50mls Glenkinchie 10 year old
Malt Whisky, or to taste*

Garnish
fresh chives, snipped into tiny pieces

To Serve
▪ Ladle into chilled bowls and garnish with snipped chives.

Variation
▪ Of course you can also serve this soup piping hot in warm soup bowls. In this case whisk a little cream until it just begins to thicken and trickle some across the top of each serving. Sprinkle the soup with snipped chives, serve and wait for the compliments.....

Cock-a-Leekie Soup

With a full bodied palate and a marked nutty finish Old Pulteney 12 year old provides yet another pleasing layer of flavour in this hearty traditional soup.

This lovely soup is mentioned in recipes as early as the 16th century and always had prunes included in the ingredients. Now-a-days it is traditional at Burns Suppers or St Andrew's Night Dinners as well as being an everyday soup for cold winters days. Some people omit the prunes though! This variation has a very special ingredient - malt whisky!

Serves 8

■ Make the marinade by mixing the whisky, tarragon, bay leaf and sugar in the water. Remove the skin from the chicken, chop up the bacon and place the chicken and bacon in a large bowl, pour over the whisky marinade, cover and leave in the refrigerator for no more than 6 hours.

■ Place the chicken mixture in a large soup pot. Chop up the leeks (reserving one for later) and onion and add to the pot with lots of salt and black pepper. Bring to the boil, cover and simmer for two hours, removing any scum it forms and adding more water if necessary.

■ Remove the chicken from the pot, allow it to cool slightly then remove the bones and chop the meat into smallish pieces and return them to the pot. Now add the rice and the last chopped leek and simmer for 30 minutes, then just before serving add the prunes and warm through.

■ Check for flavour adding more seasoning and whisky as you wish and then serve with a little chopped parsley.

Marinade
120mls Old Pulteney 12 year old Malt Whisky
1 teaspoon chopped fresh tarragon
1 large bay leaf
1 teaspoon brown sugar
2 litres water
1.5kg boiling chicken (giblets removed)
3 rashers of streaky bacon
1kg leeks, thoroughly washed
1 large onion,
salt and freshly ground black pepper
30g long grain rice
6-12 ready to eat stoned prunes
fresh flat leaf parsley, finely chopped

Woodland Mushroom Soup

Royal Lochnagar 12 year old is a perfect match for wild mushrooms, its nutty undertones bring out the woodland flavours.

This is a very rich soup using delicious wild mushrooms, dried and fresh. You can vary the mushrooms to suit what is available or your preference.

Serves 6

- Place the dried mushrooms in a bowl with the 275mls hot water and allow to stand for 30 minutes to reconstitute. Strain through a fine sieve into a bowl reserving the liquid as well as the mushrooms. Melt the butter and olive oil in a large pan, add the onion and garlic and fry gently for a few minutes until the onions have softened. Add the fresh wild mushrooms and cook for about 4 minutes. Add the reconstituted mushrooms and almost all of the mushroom liquid, avoiding any bits of grit at the bottom of the bowl. Add the wine, whisky, stock and thyme and bring to the boil. Cook for about 15 minutes until it has reduced by a half.

- Stir in the wholegrain mustard and season well. Taste and add a little more whisky if desired.

To Serve

- Ladle into warmed soup bowls and sprinkle a little chopped parsley around the edge. Serve the grated parmesan separately if serving.

Variation

- Before adding the mustard, ladle half the soup into a food processor or liquidiser and blend until smooth, then add back to the soup pan, stir in and reheat. Add the wholegrain mustard and seasoning and serve.

20g dried porcini mushrooms or a mixture of dried woodland mushrooms

275mls hot water

50g unsalted butter

a little olive oil for frying

1 large red onion, chopped quite small

3 plump cloves of garlic, crushed

125g chanterelles or mixed fresh woodland mushrooms, trimmed

120mls red wine

50mls Royal Lochnagar 12 year old Malt Whisky

1 litre dark vegetable stock (page 145)

1 tablespoon chopped fresh thyme

1 level teaspoon wholegrain mustard

salt and freshly ground black pepper

Garnish

fresh flat leaf parsley, chopped

a little grated Parmesan cheese (optional)

Creamy Mushroom and Brie Soup

This delicately flavoured soup is best improved with a malt of similar character, The Glenlivet 15 year old French Oak Reserve's creamy, rich character marries well with this soup's creamy, cheesy core flavours.

This tasty soup is always a big hit but when you add The Glenlivet you have something even more special. Try it with Scottish Brie if you can get it.

Serves 8

■ Begin by melting the butter with the olive oil in a large pan. Now add the shallots and garlic and sauté on a low heat until soft but not browned then add the mushrooms and cook them until softened.

■ Next add the stock, wine, whisky, thyme bring to the boil and reduce by half, add the cream and brie and reduce to the desired consistency.

■ Remove the sprig of thyme, liquidise the soup lightly and season with salt and lots of black pepper.

Fantastic!

1 tablespoon olive oil and a little butter
5-6 chopped shallots
8 cloves garlic crushed
600g chopped mushrooms
1 litre vegetable stock
250mls red wine
60mls Glenlivet 15 year old French Oak Reserve Malt Whisky
1 large sprig thyme
(or 2 large pinches of dried thyme)
1/2 litre double cream
300g brie with any thick skin removed
salt and freshly ground black pepper

Scotch Onion Soup

Cragganmore 12 year old's complex flavour and malty finish provides a subtle background layer to the rich flavours of this soup.

This is our version of French Onion Soup, which I think you will agree is greatly enhanced by the addition of Cragganmore. Wonderful comfort food on a chilly autumn or winter's day!

Serves 8

■ Heat the olive oil in a large pan and fry the onions for 10 minutes stirring constantly until the onions are soft and beginning to brown at the edges. When the onions are cooked add the sugar, salt and pepper and fry for a further 20 minutes, until the onions are a deep golden brown, but do not let them burn. Continue to stir and scrape the dark bits off the bottom of the pan.
■ Now add the garlic, lemon juice, beef stock, red wine, bouquet garni and the whisky. Bring to a simmer and cook for ½ hour. Add the marmite or yeast extract and taste for seasoning. You will probably need to add more salt.

1 tablespoon olive oil

1kg onions, thinly sliced, (I like to use a few red onions mixed with the brown)

20g sugar

salt and freshly ground black pepper

2 cloves of garlic, crushed

1 teaspoon lemon juice

1.5 litres beef stock

285mls red wine

1 bouquet garni

30mls Cragganmore 12 year old Malt Whisky

1 tip of a teaspoon marmite / yeast extract

To Garnish
■ Cut small slices of French baguette and toast them, drizzle each slice with olive oil and top with grated cheese. Place under the grill to melt the cheese and use to garnish each bowl of soup.

Garnish
french baguette
olive oil
200g grated cheddar cheese

To Serve
■ Serve in warm bowls and top with a slice of cheesy toast.

Velouté of Haggis laced with Glenfarclas

Glenfarclas 15 year old has a delicious oak character with a lightly smoked finish that is not going to be lost in the spiciness of the haggis.

This innovative soup was Graham's award winning starter in the Spirit of Speyside Chef of the Year 2007 competition and has an amazing depth of flavour.

Serves 4

- Over a high heat, reduce the stock by half then add the whisky and reduce by half again. Next add the haggis broken into small pieces and add honey to taste. Stir, breaking up the haggis, bring the soup to a simmer and add 200ml of the double cream. As the haggis melts it will thicken the soup.
- Now season to taste and add half of the parsley just before serving.

To Serve

- Ladle the soup into warmed bowls and garnish with a sprinkle of parsley and a swirl of the remaining cream. Your guests will be astonished!

750ml good beef stock- preferably home made

100ml Glenfarclas 15 year old Malt Whisky

400g haggis, if possible choose quite a spicy haggis or just choose your favourite

approximately 1 tablespoon heather honey, to taste

250ml double cream

salt and freshly ground black pepper for seasoning

Garnish

1 handful of fresh, finely chopped flat leaf parsley

Creamy Fish Brose

The legendary Islay malt, Ardbeg 10 year old provides a subtle background layer of taste to this classically Scottish soup. It brings a hint of smokiness which adds interest but is not enough to overpower the haddock. It also provides a gentle hint of liquorice for those who can spot it. Brose is traditionally a mixture of oatmeal, butter and salt that is often stirred into a soup. Try it with potato and leek soup! In this recipe we have married it with haddock, the favourite white fish of the Scots and that other great favourite, malt whisky! This makes a fine lunch as it is a meal in itself and it would work equally well with any white fish. As my Dad, Jack Beatt, was a wholesale fish merchant in Dundee we were privileged to have the most wonderful fresh fish when we were growing up. He also loved oatmeal so I think he would have really enjoyed this dish.

Serves 6-8

1 medium leek
1 medium onion
3 carrots
2 sticks of celery
¹/₂ small swede (neep)
50g butter plus a little olive oil
75g medium oatmeal
1 litre fish, chicken or vegetable stock
50mls Ardbeg10 year old Malt Whisky
1kg haddock fillets, check for bones and cut into pieces
salt and freshly ground black pepper
300mls double cream

Garnish
fresh chives

Without cutting through the root, cut the leek lengthwise in half and half again, and wash thoroughly then finely slice it, using the white and pale green parts. Set aside the tougher dark green leaves and the root and use them for stock. Now peel and slice the onion finely and cut the carrot in half lengthwise and then slice it thinly into bite sized pieces. Clean and destring the celery and slice them finely into similar sized pieces. Cut the swede into pieces, peel and then slice finely so that all the pieces of vegetables are about the same size. Melt the butter in a large pan with the olive oil, add all the vegetables and sweat gently with the lid on for 5 minutes. Do not allow to brown.

Now stir in the oatmeal and cook for a further 5 minutes. Add the stock and bring back to the boil, stirring continuously. Reduce the heat and simmer for 10 minutes, stirring occasionally, then add the whisky and the fish, season with salt and pepper and cook gently for a further 10 minutes. Now gently stir in the cream and heat through. Finally check the seasoning and add more whisky as desired.

To Serve
Ladle into warmed bowls, garnish with chives and serve with crusty oatmeal bread or our superb whisky soda bread. (page 206)

A very special soup …..mmm…!

Shellfish Broth laced with Caol Ila Single Malt Scotch Whisky™

The Caol Ila 12 year old's smoky taste and long sweet and sour finish provides a delicious background note to this wonderful broth.
You can use frozen shellfish for this recipe if fresh is not available.
Provide a finger bowl and a dish for the discarded shells if there are any.

Serves 4

■ Heat olive oil in a large saucepan, add the onions, garlic and chilli then cook until the onions are softened but not brown. Now add the tinned tomatoes, whisky and stock and cook for 5 minutes, then add the shellfish and cook for no more than 5 minutes.

To Serve
■ Garnish with chopped parsley and serve hot, in warm bowls with warm crusty bread to mop up the soup.

2 tablespoons olive oil
2 medium onions peeled and diced
2 cloves garlic, peeled and crushed
$^1/_2$ red chilli, deseeded and chopped finely
1 x 400g tin chopped tomatoes
60mls Caol Ila 12 year old Malt Whisky
250mls vegetable or fish stock
400g mixed shellfish; mussels, prawns, scallops, clams, squid etc. Defrosted if frozen

Garnish
fresh flat leaf parsley, finely chopped

Soups and Starters

Partan Bree

Tomatin 12 year old's complex bouquet and fruity, slightly nutty background introduces a subtle layer of flavour to this classically Scottish soup.

Partan Bree is the traditional name in Scotland for Crab Soup. "Partan" is Gaelic for crab and Brigh, pronounced "bree" is Gaelic for juice, soup or gravy. It is a wonderful, creamy, luxurious soup and with the addition of Tomatin 12 year old and the dash of Tabasco it has a little kick as well.

Serves 4

In separate bowls marinate both white and brown crab meat in a little of the whisky and set aside for no more than 20 minutes. Meanwhile boil the rice in the milk until soft but not overcooked. Now liquidise the rice and milk with the brown crab meat and some of the stock.

Return to a clean pan, add the rest of the stock and bring to the boil. Add the anchovy purée, the white crab meat, the cream and the remaining whisky and season with salt and pepper to taste. Don't be surprised, it will need quite a bit of salt. Warm through gently and when hot, serve garnished with a sprinkle of the chopped chives and spring onion plus a drop of Tabasco. *Wow!*

250g cooked crab meat
90mls Tomatin 12 year old Malt Whisky
50g long grain rice
400mls full cream milk
275mls crab, fish or chicken stock
$1/2$ teaspoon anchovy puree
200mls double cream
salt and freshly ground black pepper

Garnish
1 spring onion, very finely sliced
fresh chives, finely chopped
4 drops Tabasco

Soups and Starters

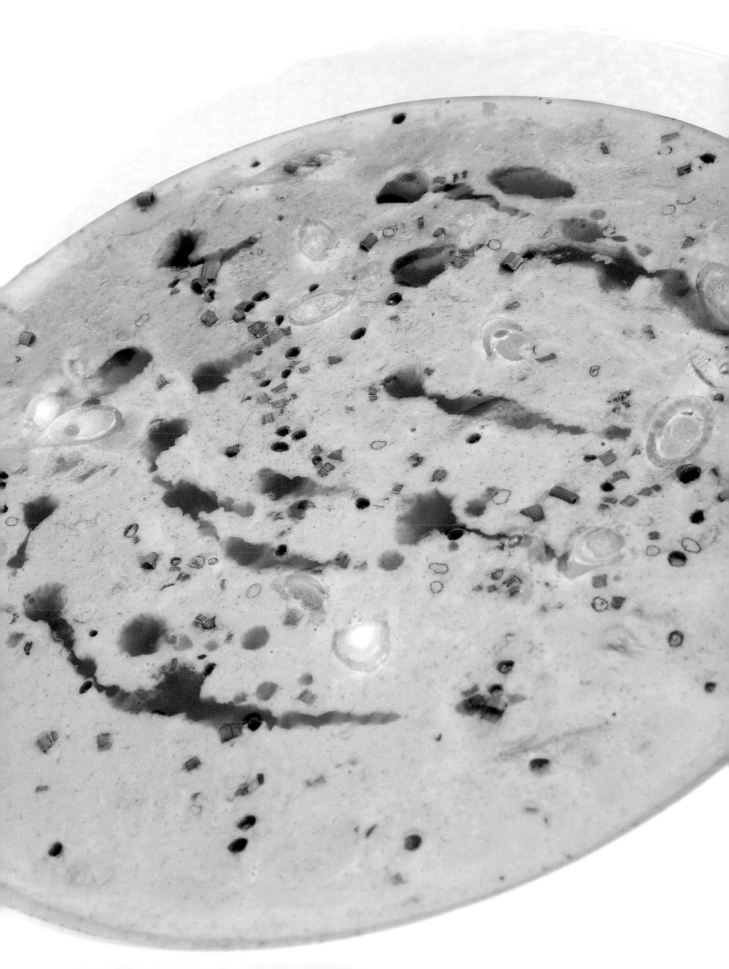

Haggis Eggs with Balmoral Sauce

Once again the oaky, slightly smoky Glenfarclas 15 year old is the perfect foil for the spicy haggis.

These little haggis "eggs" make a very tasty and unusual canapé. You could also serve them as a starter: make them a little bigger and serve on a nest of rocket leaves with the Balmoral Sauce drizzled around the plate.

Serves 8

Haggis Eggs

- Lightly whisk the egg white and set aside whilst you prepare the haggis.
- Place the haggis in a mixing bowl and break it up a little, now add the egg yolk and the whisky and mix well together, this is easiest with your hands.
- Now take teaspoonfuls of the mixture and roll into balls about the size of marbles. Don't make them too big as they are intended to be eaten in one bite. Dip each one into the lightly beaten egg white, roll in oatmeal and set on a cling filmed tray. This is slightly less messy if you try to use one hand for this task and dip them all in the egg white first then tackle the oatmeal, or wear a pair of food safe polythene gloves! You can place the tray in the fridge or freezer until you need to cook them.
- To cook, deep fry them at 180C for about 1 minute (3 minutes if cooking from frozen), until crisp and brown. Drain well on kitchen paper, insert cocktail sticks and serve hot.

Balmoral Sauce

- Bring the beef stock to the boil and reduce by a half then add the whisky and reduce again by about one third, add the honey and season to taste with salt and pepper. Finish with a knob of butter when you ready to serve. This will thicken your sauce slightly and give it a glaze.

To Serve

- Serve as a canapé with Balmoral Sauce as a dip, or serve on a nest of rocket leaves with the Balmoral Sauce drizzled around the plate.

Haggis Eggs
1 egg, separated
250g haggis
25mls Glenfarclas 15 year old Malt Whisky
250g medium or pinhead oatmeal
vegetable oil for deep frying

Balmoral Sauce
500mls beef stock
25mls Glenfarclas 15 year old Malt Whisky
15mls runny honey
salt and freshly ground black pepper
butter

Baked Figs with Lanark Blue Cheese and Parma Ham

The faintly nutty, dried fruit background of Edradour 10 year old backed up by a creamy mellow finish give this dressing a powerful edge and perfectly balances the strong blue cheese. A few generations ago my Dad's family farmed the land beside the tiny Edradour Distillery. It is situated in the hills above Pitlochry and is a magical spot, well worth a visit, you will love it.

This is a gorgeous, rather stylish starter that is easy to prepare in advance and quick to cook. It tastes absolutely divine! It'll get your taste buds tingling, what a start to a meal!

Serves 4

Preheat oven to 180C/Gas 4

- Carefully cut a cross in the top of each fig and gently press open. Divide the cheese between the figs, wrap Parma ham around each fig and secure with cocktail sticks. Mix the honey and whisky together and drizzle a little on top of each fig and place on a baking sheet* and bake in the oven for about 5 minutes until the Parma ham is crispy and the cheese has melted.
- Meanwhile, make the dressing by whisking all the dressing ingredients together, or place them in a jar with a lid and shake until they are combined.
- Dress some mixed salad leaves and place them in the centre of each plate. Place 2 figs on top of each salad, remove the cocktail sticks, place a spoonful of red onion marmalade (page 141) on the plate and sprinkle a few chopped walnuts around.

You can prepare the figs to this stage in the morning and then bake them when you are ready to serve.

Variations
- If you can't get Lanark Blue Cheese, try using your favourite blue cheese. Strathdon Blue, Roquefort and Gorgonzola are all lovely in this recipe. They each bring their own individual qualities and flavours, so you can ring the changes.
- If you are not a blue cheese fan, try it with Goats Cheese   mmm.....
- Vegetarians can simply omit the Parma ham, it is still lovely.

8 figs, ripe but not overly ripe

150g Lanark Blue Cheese

8 slices Parma ham

15mls runny honey

5mls Edradour 10 year old Malt Whisky

Dressing

10mls Edradour 10 year old Malt Whisky, or to taste

1 tablespoon red wine vinegar

3 tablespoons olive oil

1 teaspoon honey

Garnish

mixed salad leaves to serve

red onion marmalade

4 chopped walnut halves

Haggis Balmoral

A wonderful little starter with the classic combination of haggis, neeps and tatties but served with a tasty whisky sauce. This dish has always been a winner in our restaurants.

Serves 4

400g floury potatoes like Maris Piper, peeled and quartered

225g swede (neep), peeled and chopped into small chunks

25g butter for the potatoes plus a little for the neeps

30mls cream

salt and freshly ground black pepper

350g haggis

300mls Whisky Madeira Sauce see page 142. You can choose the plain or the creamy version both are lovely with this dish

Garnish

4 sprigs of heather or parsley

You will need four 6cm mousse rings 7cm high or make your own from plastic piping (see page 166).

■ Place the potatoes in a pan of cold water, sufficient to just cover the potatoes, add salt and bring to the boil. Cook until tender, about 10-15 minutes, drain and return to the hot pan for a few minutes to dry out. Add the butter and cream and mash until smooth, season to taste. Set aside and keep warm. At the same time place the chopped neep in boiling salted water until tender, about 15 minutes, drain and return to the hot pan to dry. Add a small knob of butter and a pinch of sugar and season well to taste. Set aside and keep warm.

■ Meanwhile make the Whisky Madeira Sauce and set it aside. When you are ready to serve, break the haggis up, place it in a bowl and heat in the microwave for 1 minute or more depending on the wattage of your microwave. Do not overheat. Alternatively, spread the haggis out in a casserole dish, cover with a lid or tinfoil and place in the oven at 190C/Gas 5 until heated through, about 15 minutes, but check it and stir the haggis occasionally.

■ Now assemble the dish. Place a ring on each plate and divide the mashed potato between them and press down. Add a layer of haggis and press down neatly, finally top with the mashed neep and smooth the top. Remove the rings, pour the sauce around the stacks and top with a sprig of heather or parsley.

Looks and tastes great!

Variation

■ For a change you could replace the Whisky Madeira Sauce with the Balmoral Sauce on page 31.

Glenfiddich® Chicken Liver Pâté

Chicken liver pâté is frequently flavoured with brandy, but just try it infused with Glenfiddich and you'll be amazed at how wonderful it tastes. The chopped green peppercorns add a fantastic punch and the whole peppercorn garnish makes it look very pretty.
Ideally you need to cook this wonderful smooth pâté the day before, to give it time to chill and set before serving.

Serves 8

■ First check the chicken livers for gall bladder (green bits) and remove them because they are very bitter. Now start by melting the butter in a pan and fry the shallots very gently until transparent. You must not allow to them to brown. Increase the heat and add the livers, garlic, thyme, salt and pepper and cook briefly until the liver begins to change colour. Add the port, lemon juice and whisky and cook gently until the liver is only just cooked. It is important not to cook it for too long or the liver will become tough.

■ Whilst the liver is cooking chop the drained green peppercorns quite finely. Do this slowly and carefully otherwise they will be all over the kitchen! Once you get a few chopped it becomes easier. Set them aside.

■ When the liver is cooked and this only takes a few minutes, add the cream and simmer until it reduces a little, and then scrape the mixture into a food processor and purée until very smooth. If you want to make it even smoother pass it through a sieve or a mouli.

■ Finally stir in the chopped peppercorns and check the seasoning. Turn the mixture into a container and cool quickly over a bowl of ice. When it is cooled, cover and place in the fridge to set, this will take 2-3 hours. The pâté will now keep for about 4 days in a sealed container.

500g chicken livers
50g butter
120g shallots roughly chopped
1 plump clove of garlic, crushed
1 heaped teaspoonful of fresh thyme leaves or ¹/₂ level teaspoon dried thyme
1¹/₂ teaspoons salt
a few turns of freshly ground black pepper
15mls port wine
1 teaspoon lemon juice
15mls Glenfiddich 12 year old Malt Whisky
2 level teaspoons green peppercorns (peppercorns in brine) plus a few extra for garnishing
75mls double cream

To Serve

■ If you are serving it as soon as it has set, fill an individual ramekin with the pâté, top with 3 green peppercorns and serve with dressed salad leaves and a spoonful of red onion marmalade on the side. (page 141) Lovely with melba toast, crusty bread or oatcakes.

■ The pâté can be pressed into individual pâté dishes or a terrine and then after it has set, topped with melted butter. This will keep it fresh for 2 weeks in the fridge. You can also serve the pâté by creating a quenelle using two spoons and passing the pâté from spoon to spoon until you have a lovely oval shape or scoop it using an ice cream scoop and top with the green peppercorns as above.

Venison and Pork Terrine

The rich berry and dried fruit flavours backed by some spiciness of Benromach 21 year old marry well with all the layers of flavours in this rich terrine.

This lovely rustic terrine looks impressive but it is very simple to assemble and cook. It is absolutely delicious with crusty bread, pickles and chutney or as we have served it here, with Apple and Rosehip Jelly. Don't be intimidated by the long list of ingredients, it is incredibly easy and well worth it!

Serves 8

Preheat oven to 180C/Gas 4

Ideally you need to start this dish the day before because it needs to chill and be pressed in the fridge for several hours.

■ Heat the olive oil in a frying pan and gently fry the onion until it is soft and transparent, add the garlic and cook for about a minute. While the onion is cooking put the venison into the food processor and pulse just a couple of times so that the meat stays coarsely chopped. Empty into a large bowl and set aside. Repeat with the kidneys, pork and bacon, all roughly chopped and added to the bowl. Add the onion and garlic, and all the remaining ingredients except the liver and mix it all together. I think that it is easier to evenly distribute all the ingredients if you use your hands.

■ Put half of the mixture into the tin and lay the sliced liver lengthways on top. Cover with the remaining mixture, it should be slightly rounded on top. Cover with tinfoil or a terrine lid. Place in a roasting tin in the oven and pour boiling water around it to come halfway up the sides of the tin. Cook for 1½ hours. Remove from the oven, uncover and put it back in the oven for a further 15 minutes until the top is lightly browned.

■ Remove from the oven and if there is a lot of liquid pour some away then cover again with tinfoil or greaseproof paper, top this with a piece of cardboard cut to fit the terrine then place a few unopened tins of food on top to compact it. As soon as it is cool enough, refrigerate for at least 4 hours, preferably overnight. The terrine will taste better if it is allowed to stay refrigerated for at least 24 hours, then remove and allow it to come to room temperature before serving it.

To Serve

■ About 30 minutes before serving, carefully tip out any remaining liquid around the terrine, run a knife around the sides of the terrine to loosen it and then to turn it out of the tin, place a chopping board on top, hold the terrine steady and quickly turn the whole thing over. Now lift the tin off the terrine. Cut the required number of slices ½ inch / 1 cm thick and place them on to the serving plates, sprinkle with a little sea salt. (Cover the remaining terrine in cling film and return to the fridge, where it will keep for up to 2 weeks.)

■ Serve with a few dressed salad leaves, a spoonful of apple and rosehip jelly (page 146), a few pickles and some warm crusty bread, now imagine the sun is shining and you are in a lovely pavement café in France....... enjoy!

Variations

■ You can vary this recipe by adding a layer of finely sliced sautéed mushrooms. You could also omit the pistachios or add your favourite nuts to give that change of texture and flavour.

2 tablespoons olive oil

1 large onion, finely chopped

2 large cloves garlic, finely chopped

500g venison loin, cut into small pieces

100g lamb's kidney cut into small pieces

375g rindless, boned belly pork, cut into small pieces

125g back bacon, cut into small pieces

8 juniper berries, crushed

25g dried cranberries

50g pistachio nuts, shelled and left whole

50mls Benromach 21 year old Malt Whisky

1 teaspoon salt

freshly ground black pepper

1 teaspoon dried thyme

1 teaspoon dried rosemary, chopped finely

large handful fresh flat leaf parsley, finely chopped

1 large egg, beaten

150g lamb's liver, sliced quite thinly, with the skin and any large tubes removed

You will need a lightly greased 1kg loaf tin or terrine.

Spicy Laphroaig® Smoked Salmon Pots

The peat smoke and seaweed aroma, in addition to the fish oil and seawater background, make Laphroaig 10 year old a perfect match for this spicy salmon dish. The flavours of the whisky come through at all levels.

This is an unusual tasty twist on a classic starter which also makes wonderful little canapés. I created this dish for my brother Gordon because Laphroaig is his favourite malt and he loves spicy food. I suggest that you make this recipe from salmon off-cuts rather than the more expensive smoked sides.

Serves 6

▨ Place all the ingredients into a food processor and blend until smooth. Check the seasoning, it may need a little more lemon juice, salt or Tabasco. Now press into small ramekins and smooth the tops.

To Serve

▨ Place the pot on a plate with a few baby salad leaves, a wedge of lemon and melba toast, warm crusty oatmeal bread, whisky soda bread (page 206) or oatcakes. This mixture also makes delicious little canapés when piped or spooned on to tiny biscuits, baby scones or into little pastry cases.

Variation

▨ If you are not serving these little pots immediately, melt some unsalted butter and pour it over the tops of the ramekins. Now that the salmon pots are sealed they will keep for up to 2 weeks in the fridge.

225g smoked salmon off-cuts

180g soft cheese e.g. Crowdie or Philadelphia

15mls Laphroaig 10 year old Malt Whisky

1 heaped tablespoon of mixed finely chopped fresh herbs – parsley, chives, chervil, dill and tarragon

20mls lemon juice

10mls horseradish sauce

about 10 drops of Tabasco or more to taste

you may need a little salt, but check first because the smoked salmon will be salty.

Optional for sealing
50g unsalted butter

BenRiach Smoked Mackerel Pâté

BenRiach's Dark Rum Wood 15 year old's clean and refreshing initial taste, spicy and rummy background and citrus finish is just the perfect match for all the ingredients in this pâté. This is a lovely simple recipe which is quite sublime.

Serves 4 – 6

■ Place all the ingredients in a food processor and whizz until smooth. Empty into a bowl and chill over a bowl of ice. *Now how easy is that?*

To Serve
■ Once chilled, pack the pâté into individual ramekins or serve a spoonful on each serving dish, either way serve with salad leaves, capers, a slice of lemon and toasted wholemeal bread and maybe a spoonful of apple chutney, sliced apple, rhubarb and ginger chutney (page 143) or red onion marmalade (page 141).

350g smoked mackerel

2 thick slices of brown bread

*25mls cider vinegar
(or white wine vinegar)*

30mls BenRiach Dark Rum Wood 15 year old Malt Whisky

100g Granny Smith apple, peeled and cored (or other sharp tasting eating apple)

1 pinch cayenne pepper

Seared Scallops with Tullibardine™ Cream

With a slightly buttery background, perhaps also a hint of nuts, backed up by a delicately spiced finish, Tullibardine Single Malt provides a perfect match for the warm flavour of the celeriac puree, the spicy black pudding and the sweet scallops.

When you are buying scallops, make sure the meat has not been previously frozen or bulked out by the addition of water. This can account for 40% of the weight of the scallop and you will be really disappointed when you try to cook it. If you can source hand-dived scallops this is better for the environment, otherwise ask your fishmonger for dry king scallops.

Serves 4

300g celeriac root, peeled and cut into small cubes
25g unsalted butter
salt and freshly ground black pepper
250mls double cream
juice of ¹/₂ lemon
15mls Tullibardine Single Malt Whisky
12 slices of black pudding, cut to about the same diameter as the scallops
12 king scallops, ask your fishmonger to remove them from the shells
oil and unsalted butter for frying

▢ First prepare the celeriac mash. Add the cubes of celeriac to a pan of boiling, salted water and cook for ten minutes until soft, drain and return to the hot pan to boil off the residual water. Mash to a smooth purée with the unsalted butter, season to taste and set aside to keep warm.

▢ Over a medium heat bring the double cream and lemon juice to a simmer and add the whisky, simmer to reduce to a thick cream. Season to taste.

▢ Clean the scallops by removing the hard "foot" and the orange coral and membrane around the outside of the flesh. Set aside the coral. Dry the scallops on a kitchen towel and sprinkle with a little salt and freshly ground black pepper. Some people prefer not to use the corals as they are a stronger taste than the scallop meat, we love them so we like to cook them and let the diner decide.

▢ Place two large heavy based frying pans on a high heat for a few minutes. Add a little oil and a small knob of butter to the hot frying pans, put the black pudding in one of the pans and fry, turning once until cooked through. Meanwhile add the scallops to the other pan, they must sizzle when they touch the surface of the pan otherwise your pan is not hot enough. Do not move them around the surface of the pan, as this will prevent the caramelisation of the surface of the scallop. After 1 – 2 minutes turn the scallops and add the coral to the pan, cook for about 30 seconds, turn the corals and turn off the heat.

To Serve

▢ Working quickly, place three small spoonfuls of the celeriac mash on each warmed serving plate, top this with a slice of the black pudding, then top with a scallop and the coral. Drizzle a little sauce around each plate and serve immediately.

Variation

▢ Just before serving, whisk the sauce in a jug with a hand blender to create a foam and drizzle it on the plate for a very modern "cheffy" presentation.

Mussel Tart

Hazelburn 8 year old's complex background and what I can only describe as a hint of sea spray are perfect matches for this luscious tart.

Serve this delicate tart as a starter or a main course; it makes a wonderful dinner party dish but would be equally at home as a lunch or supper dish. It radiates sunshine and tastes as good as it looks.

Preheat oven to 200C/Gas 6

■ For the pastry, sieve flour and salt into a bowl. Rub in the butter and lard until a breadcrumb texture is achieved. Now cutting into the mixture with a knife, add the water gradually, cutting and turning until it comes together to a soft dough, adding more water if necessary. Do not over work it or you will make it tough. Turn the dough out on to a floured work surface and knead lightly, then cover in cling film and put it in the fridge and chill for 30 minutes. *It is really important to allow the dough to rest at this stage, otherwise it will be very difficult to roll and it will break and crack, ultimately making it heavy.*

■ Roll the pastry out larger than the size of your tart case and lift it using the rolling pin, carefully ease it into the tin, do not stretch it or it will shrink back when baked, gently press it on to the base and sides. Cut away any excess so that the edges come slightly above the top edge of the tin then crimp the edges with your fingers and the blunt edge of a knife. If you are using a fluted tart tin, run a rolling pin over the edges to cut off the excess.

■ Prick the base gently, cover with grease proof paper and add the baking beans. Rest for 15 minutes in the fridge then bake for 10-15 minutes until the pastry is set but not browned. Take the tart out of the oven and remove the beans and greaseproof paper. Reduce the oven heat to 180C/Gas 4 for a further 5 minutes or until the base begins to brown and crisp.

■ Pour the wine and whisky into a large pan with a lid, add the cleaned mussels, half of the thyme and one quarter of the chopped parsley. Cook on a medium heat with the lid on until the mussels are cooked and open (3 to 4 minutes). Drain the mussels, retaining the liquor. Shell the mussels and set them aside. Discard any mussels that have not opened.

■ Add the butter and oil to a saucepan, heat and then sweat off the shallots and garlic on a low to medium heat for 4 to 5 minutes. Add half of the reserved mussel liquor and the lemon juice and reduce rapidly until most of the liquid is gone. This will take about 15 minutes. Set this reduction aside to cool.

■ Now beat the egg yolks lightly with the cream, the remaining chopped parsley, thyme, grated lemon zest, salt and pepper. Add the cooled reduction and stir it in. Taste to check the seasoning.

■ Sprinkle the mussels on the pastry case and pour over the mixture then bake in the oven for 15 to 20 minutes until the egg mix is just set. Remove from the oven and allow to it to cool a little in the tin.

To Serve

■ This tart can be served cold, but is particularly light and luscious when it is served warm.

■ Dress a handful of rocket and watercress with vinaigrette and place on each plate alongside a portion of the tart with a swirl of saffron sauce. If it is a main course serve with boiled new potatoes, steamed asparagus and saffron sauce.

Serves 6 – 10

Shortcrust Pastry
225g plain flour, (plus a little for 'dusting')
pinch salt
60g unsalted butter, cut roughly into small pieces
60g lard, cut into pieces
2 tablespoon ice cold water

Tart Filling
1 bottle (750mls) dry white wine
60mls Hazelburn 8 year old Malt Whisky
1kg mussels, cleaned (page 122)
1 large bunch of fresh flat leaf parsley, chopped
a few sprigs of fresh thyme with the leaves stripped off or 2 pinches dried thyme
40g butter and a little olive oil
5-8 shallots, chopped
5 plump cloves of garlic, crushed
the juice and grated zest of 1 small lemon
6 large egg yolks
325mls double cream
salt and freshly ground black pepper to season

To Serve
rocket leaves
1 bunch watercress
vinaigrette salad dressing – 2 tablespoons olive oil, juice of ¹/₂ lemon, pinch sugar, whisked together
saffron sauce (page 142)
fresh flat leaf parsley, chopped, to garnish

You will need a lightly greased 22cm loose bottomed tart case.

Soups and Starters

Twice Baked Arbroath Smokie Soufflés

Served with Talisker™ and Anchovy Cream

Talisker 12 year old's pungent aroma, peppery flavour and big finish are not lost when placed against the strong flavours of the smoked fish and the anchovies.

These soufflés are brilliant because you can make them up to 2 days in advance and keep them in the fridge until you are ready to serve them.

I suggest that you double the quantities and freeze a few away for a treat later. My Mum used to make Smokie Soufflé regularly and she used a family sized soufflé dish and served it straight away, which you can do as well of course. The recipe will adjust to fit the size of your family.

Lightly grease 6 ramekins.   *Preheat oven to 180C/Gas 4*

■ Place the milk, shallots, bay leaves, blade of mace and peppercorns in a pan and slowly bring to the boil, this will take about 5 minutes. Set aside for a few minutes for the milk to absorb the flavours then strain into a bowl and discard the flavourings.

■ Since the Smokies are hot smoked, they can be eaten without any further cooking, so all you need to do to remove the flesh from the fish is to warm it slightly either in the microwave, a steamer or wrap it in tinfoil and place in the oven for 5 minutes. Split the fish open and remove the back bone, it comes away very easily from the tail end, and the flesh can be flaked, taking care to avoid the bones. Set this aside.

■ Now, gently melt the butter in a pan, do not allow it to brown or you will spoil the taste of the sauce, and then stir in the flour, stir quickly with a wooden spoon, making a paste (a roux). Cook the roux gently for a minute or so then gradually add the warm milk stirring all the time until the mixture is smooth and thick. Now turn the heat right down and allow the sauce to simmer for 3 minutes to cook out the flour, stirring or whisking occasionally. Next stir in the grated cheese and cook for a few minutes until the cheese is melted.

■ Now transfer the sauce to a large bowl and leave it to cool slightly. Whisk the egg whites until they form stiff peaks and set aside while you whisk the egg yolks lightly and add them to the sauce, mix until well blended and season with salt and black pepper. Add the flaked fish, taking care not to break the fish up too much; you want the flakes to stay as intact as possible.

■ Gradually fold the egg whites into the cheesy fish mixture, do not stir or you will lose the air from the egg whites. Check the seasoning and then divide between the ramekins and place in a roasting tin with enough hot water to come half way up the ramekins. Bake for about 35-40 minutes until well risen, firm and becoming golden brown.

Serves 4 - 6

250ml full cream milk

2 shallots, cut in half

1 bay leaf

6 black peppercorns

1 blade of mace

60g flaked Arbroath Smokie (if you can't get these wonderful fish and they are worth the effort, the recipe will work with cold smoked haddock, buy the pale traditionally smoked though, not the bright yellow dyed version)

25g butter

25g self raising flour

25g cheddar cheese (or gruyere), grated

4 large eggs, separated

1 extra egg white

Talisker™ and Anchovy Cream

250mls double cream

10mls Talisker 12 year old Malt Whisky

25mls of anchovy paste

Depending on the size of the ramekins this mixture will make 4-6 soufflés.

Twice Baked Arbroath Smokie Soufflés *(continued)*

▢ You can serve these soufflés immediately or you can place them in the fridge and re-bake any time within 2 days. Allow them to cool slightly but not completely or you will have trouble getting them cleanly out of the ramekins (they will sink a bit but don't worry) and then loosen from the ramekins by running the blade of a knife around the sides, pat the bottom and give them a shake, they should come out quite cleanly. If they don't, and they are still warm leave them for another few minutes. Now turn them out upside down on to a cling filmed tray, *easiest if you shake the soufflé out onto your hand first then gently lay on the tray.* At this stage they can be covered and refrigerated. They also freeze very well and once defrosted just follow the instructions below.

When you want to serve them   *Preheat oven to 200C/Gas 6*
▢ Lightly grease a baking tray and place the soufflés on it, the right way up again. Bake for 10 minutes or until they have risen again and have become light and fluffy. *They will not rise as much as originally but they will be very light.* Now, you need to serve them immediately, so you need to make the Anchovy and Talisker Cream while the soufflés are in the oven.

To Serve
▢ Trickle some Talisker and Anchovy Cream across the plates and set some baby salad leaves to one side, dress the salad with olive oil and balsamic vinegar and at the last moment place a soufflé on each plate. Serve immediately and wait for the compliments.......

Arbroath Smokies are a type of lightly smoked small haddock which are a speciality of the town of Arbroath in Angus Scotland. They are hot smoked and are prepared using traditional methods dating back to the late 1800s. They have a quite different taste to the more readily available cold smoked haddock. In 2004 the European Commission registered the designation "Arbroath Smokies" as a Protected Geographical Indication under the EU's Protected Food Name Scheme, acknowledging its unique status.

Talisker™ and Anchovy Cream
▢ Combine all the ingredients and whisk until just beginning to thicken. Taste and add more anchovy paste or whisky to your preference.

Some people will say that they don't like anchovies, but they just give this cream a wonderful savoury taste. Try it!

Islay Angels

Bunnahabhain 12 year old is not as smoky as its Islay neighbours and the sweet undertones complement this dish perfectly.

Oysters with cheese and bacon is a classic combination and here we have used smoked cheddar which brings a wonderful flavour to this dish and works so well with the whisky. This is a delightful canapé or very posh starter served with a dram of Bunnahabhain. Wonderful for a wedding breakfast!

Serves 4

First place the oysters in a bowl with the whisky and allow them to marinate for no longer than 20 minutes. Pat the oysters dry with some kitchen paper and place each one on a piece of cheese, wrap it tightly with the bacon and secure it with a cocktail stick. Now place them under a hot grill until the bacon is crisp, turning once and then serve immediately.

12 oysters

15mls Bunnahabhain 12 year old Malt Whisky

50g smoked cheddar cheese, cut into 12 cubes

6 rashers rindless streaky bacon, cut in half

Variations

You can create several very different dishes by varying the cheese or by using smoked oysters which incidentally, are fabulous. You can also use pancetta instead of the streaky bacon.

Scottish Gravadlax

Here are two of our favourite Whisky cured salmon recipes, the first is my brother Gordon's speciality and the other one is our invention and one we have served many times in the Restaurant. They are both wonderful and I am sure you will enjoy them as much as we do. Once cured in this way the salmon will keep for a week in the fridge. You can serve them both together as a Duo of Gravadlax. Very impressive!

Gordon's Special Speyside Cure

■ Rub the honey, whisky, orange juice and peel over salmon. Combine the sugar, salt and dill and cover both sides of each piece of the salmon.* Place one fillet, skin side down in a ceramic or glass bowl or plate, top with the other fillet skin side up, with the thick end against the other's thin end. Wrap in cling film, cover with a chopping board and place weights on top, a couple of unused cans of food are fine, and allow to marinate in the fridge for two days if the fillets are thick, 24 hours if they are thin. Turn the fish over or baste once or twice during this time. When they are ready, pour off the brine and rinse the fish under cold running water, otherwise the fish will be too salty.

Raspberry and Beetroot Ceviche

■ Crush the peppercorns in a mortar if you have one, if not place in a bowl and crush with the end of a rolling pin. Blend all of the ingredients in a food processor to form a loose paste, cover both sides of each piece of the salmon and continue as above.*

To Serve (for either recipe)

■ With a sharp knife, cut thin horizontal (or vertical) slices but don't cut through the skin. Serve as a canapé on slices of brown toast or rye bread with lemon juice and a sprinkling of dill or as a starter with a little salad, lemon wedges, capers and dill. You could also serve as a main course with new potatoes and a mustard and dill salad sauce.

Mustard and Dill Salad Sauce

■ Place all of the ingredients in a container with a tight fitting lid, replace the lid and leave for 10 minutes to allow the flavours to develop.

To Serve

■ Shake vigorously to emulsify the sauce and serve. This sauce is delicious with lots of fish dishes. Wonderful with a poached salmon salad.

Gordon's Special Speyside Cure

Aberlour 10 year old's balance of spice and orange are in perfect harmony with this Scottish twist on a classic marinade for salmon.

2 tablespoons heather honey
50mls Aberlour 10 year old Malt Whisky
juice of one or two oranges depending on their size
the peel of 1 orange
225g soft brown sugar
225g salt
a sprinkling of dried dill

Garnish

a few slices of oranges

Raspberry and Beetroot Ceviche

Talisker 12 year old provides a subtle background contrast to the cure for this exciting salmon dish

30mls Talisker 12 year old Malt Whisky
1 tablespoon mixed peppercorns
1 dessertspoon ground allspice
150g salt
150g sugar
100mls raspberry coulis (see page 166)
150g beetroot
6 tablespoons fresh dill chopped

Garnish

a few fresh raspberries

For both recipes you will need one side of salmon with skin on, descaled. Check the fish for pin bones and remove as necessary, then cut it in half.

Mustard and Dill Salad Sauce

1 tablespoon Dijon mustard
1 tablespoon caster sugar
$1/2$ teaspoon salt
1 pinch ground white pepper
1 tablespoon white wine vinegar
juice of 1 orange
6 tablespoons olive oil
6 tablespoons chopped fresh dill

Creamy Prawn Pots

Talisker 12 year old's peppery flavour and strong finish, lift this dish to new heights. This is an incredibly easy, yet very glamorous starter.

Serves 4

Start by buttering 4 ramekins lightly. Now melt the remaining butter in a pan and fry the chopped onion very gently until soft - do not brown. This will take about 3-4 minutes. Now add the prawns and heat through, quickly add the whisky and cook for a further 2 minutes. Stir in the cream and heat again but remove the mixture from the heat before it reaches boiling point. It is very important not to overcook the prawns or they will be rubbery and tasteless! Add the chopped chives and stir in.

Season to taste and spoon into the ramekins. Sprinkle the grated cheese on top and brown under a hot grill.

To Serve
Serve immediately garnished with chopped parsley and toast triangles on the side   *mmm....*

Variation
You could vary the cheese you use. Try replacing the cheddar cheese with a thin slice of goat's cheese log. You will then have a completely different dish but equally wonderful!

25g butter
2 plump shallots, finely chopped
400g medium/large raw prawns, shelled
50mls Talisker 12 yr old Malt Whisky
150mls double cream
1 teaspoon chopped fresh chives
salt and freshly ground black pepper
50g grated cheddar cheese

Garnish
fresh flat leaf parsley, finely chopped

Glazed Chanterelles with Royal Lochnagar Single Malt Scotch Whisky

The woody, nutty undertones of Royal Lochnagar 12 year old are the perfect match for any woodland mushroom but they really accentuate the flavour of chanterelles without overpowering their delicate exquisite taste.

Chanterelles are beautiful wild mushrooms which are to be found from early summer to late autumn all over Britain but they grow in great profusion in Scotland in birch and other woodland areas which have open mossy clearings. They are very highly prized because their bright, almost orange colour and pretty flowery shape give a wonderful colour and a beautiful appearance to many dishes. They have a faint scent of apricots and taste delightful. It is however, extremely important to be able to distinguish them from false chanterelles which look similar, grow in the same habitat, at the same time, but they will make you ill! If you don't have an expert to teach you, stick to buying them from your vegetable supplier.

Serves 4

25g butter
1-2 cloves garlic, crushed
1 sprig of thyme
250g chanterelles, brushed clean
15mls Royal Lochnagar 12 year old Malt Whisky
100mls double cream
1 teaspoon lemon juice
fresh flat leaf parsley, finely chopped
fresh breadcrumbs
a knob of butter

Garnish
fresh flat leaf parsley, finely chopped

■ Melt the butter in a frying pan, and gently cook the crushed garlic briefly, then add the chanterelles with the leaves stripped from the thyme and cook gently for a few minutes. Now add the whisky and turn the heat up to cook off the whisky then add the double cream and lemon juice and simmer to reduce a little. Finally sprinkle in the parsley and stir.

To Serve
■ Divide the chanterelle cream between 4 heatproof dishes, top with breadcrumbs and a little butter dotted over the top. Place under a hot grill until browned and serve immediately sprinkled with parsley and with wholemeal toast on the side.

Variations
■ You can use this recipe as the filling for a wonderful short crust pastry tart, fantastic as a starter or a main course veggie option, topped with flaked almonds instead of the breadcrumbs.

■ It's also very good without the breadcrumb topping, simply served on toast.

Lanark Blue and Caramelised Apple Pâté

Old Pulteney 12 year old's full bodied, sweet background with a finish of fresh fruit and a suggestion of salt match all aspects of this strong ewe's milk blue cheese.
This is a delicious pâté so fresh and lively, a wonderful way to start a meal.

Serves 4

■ Melt the butter in a frying pan, add the sugar and then the sliced apples and cook them over a high heat until they are caramelised but still firm and then allow them to cool.

■ Set aside 8 pieces of apple for garnishing then place the apples and all the other ingredients except the seasoning in the food processor and pulse until everything is combined but left slightly rough. Taste and season carefully.

■ Spoon the pâté into ramekins and top with a couple of slices of caramelised apple and serve with fruit chutney such as our Rhubarb and Ginger Chutney (page 143) or Red Onion Marmalade (page 141), a few pickled walnuts, a garnish of dressed baby salad leaves, finely sliced celery and wholemeal or melba toast.

15g butter

60g demerara sugar

3 sharp apples e.g. Granny Smiths, peeled, cored and sliced

225g Lanark Blue cheese (or your favourite blue cheese, Dunsyre, Strathdon or Stilton)

120g soft cheese, (or more to taste, depending on which blue cheese you use.)

$^1/_2$ spring onion, finely chopped

20mls Old Pulteney 12 year old Malt Whisky

a little salt and freshly ground black pepper

Soups and Starters

Grilled Goats Cheese with Sweet and Sour Beetroot

The Famous Grouse Blended Scotch Whisky, Scotland's best selling blend, with its fruity, lightly smoky palate with a background of toffee and spices, contrasts well with the rich goat's cheese and earthy beetroot.

This is a delightful starter which is very easy to prepare. The flavours are a little different and work so well together. Also because you can prepare so much in advance, it's perfect for a dinner party. Try it!

Serves 4

■ Slice the beetroot, reserving the liquid from the bag or box. Heat the oil in a frying pan and add the shallots and garlic and cook gently for a few minutes until the shallots are transparent, this will take 3 or 4 minutes. Now add the beetroot and stir in. Next add the vinegar, redcurrant jelly, beetroot juices and whisky and cook for a few minutes until the flavours are well combined. Now taste and season with salt and pepper and adjust the sweetness and tartness according to your taste. You will probably also have to add a little water to create a syrupy sauce.*

To Serve
■ When you are ready to serve the dish, preheat your grill to its highest setting. Toast your slices of bread and set aside, (or toast in your toaster). Now place the slices of goats cheese on an ovenproof tray and place under the hot grill until the cheese browns and just begins to melt.

■ Meanwhile, dress a handful of salad leaves with a little vinaigrette then place it in the centre of each plate and put the piece of toast on top. Divide the warm sweet and sour beetroot between each piece of toast, top each with a slice of goats cheese and trickle some balsamic reduction over the cheese and serve whilst still hot.

* You can prepare to this point several days in advance and keep the sweet and sour beetroot in an airtight container in the fridge until you wish to serve it. You will need to warm the beetroot before serving it and you may want to add a little more water as it may have dried a little in the fridge.

250g cooked beetroot (try to find the freshly cooked rather than the vacuum packed, but either will work)

5 shallots, peeled and divided into cloves or cut into chunks

1 plump clove of garlic, crushed

a little sunflower oil for frying shallots

100mls white wine vinegar

1 tablespoon redcurrant jelly

30mls Famous Grouse Blended Scotch Whisky

salt and freshly ground black pepper

a little water

4 slices walnut & raisin bread (from a good bakery or make your own)

4 slices of goats cheese log (or 4 individual crotins)

rocket or other baby salad leaves, washed

vinaigrette salad dressing

balsamic vinegar reduction

Brambles

Speyside

The River Spey is Scotland's second longest river, flowing from its source high in the hills above Loch Laggan to the Moray Coast at Spey Bay, where the river meets the sea. Speyside is one of Scotland's most beautiful regions and its name is synonymous with two of Scotland's greatest products, salmon and whisky.

This is the home of the elusive wild Atlantic salmon and some anglers who have fished here for more than 20 years still await that first fish. There are superb beats on the estates of Castle Grant and Tulchan while Town Association Waters are spaced out along the length of the river. Ghillies will endeavour to guide you to your first salmon and coach you in the art of Speycasting.

Strathspey is one of Scotland's major tourist destinations – here the river's upper reaches, sandwiched between the magnificent Cairngorm and Monadhliath mountain ranges, offer fantastic opportunities for hill walking, hiking, water sports, mountain biking and winter sports. The vast acreage of Caledonian pine forests are home to rare wildlife such as golden eagles, red squirrels, pine martens, wildcats, capercaillie, and ospreys, while Britain's only herd of wild reindeer roams freely over the Cairngorms. Whilst in this area take a trip on the funicular railway to the top of Cairngorm, the views are breathtaking. You could also visit the Reindeer Centre at Glenmore or take a walk along the sandy shores of Loch Morlich and marvel at this beautiful loch amid the mountains. On your way back to Aviemore, stop off at the Rothiemurchus Estate shop, they have a fabulous range of local produce, gifts and crafts.

Just south of Aviemore and overshadowed by the massive granite outcrops above Alvie Estate, sits Alvie Gardens, at 900ft above sea level it is the highest fruit farm in the UK. Surrounded by high walls to protect the crop, John Christie produces some of the finest strawberries, raspberries and other soft fruits you will ever taste. This family business started in 1995 and has since gone from strength to strength. Visitors will have plenty of chances to taste John's berries as, when in season, they are available in almost every outlet from Newtonmore to Grantown-on-Spey. Retailers proudly display their association with Alvie Gardens on large advertising boards announcing the availability of this season's crop.

At the heart of Speyside on the A95, just one mile south of Grantown on Spey, is Craggan Mill Restaurant. Why not pop in and sample some of the region's finest produce? We would love to see you and will happily sign a copy of this book for you.

A stone's throw beyond the restaurant is the Capital of Strathspey, Grantown-on-Spey, which marks the northern edge of the Cairngorms National Park. With the beautiful tree lined square, the Victorian and Mid-Georgian architecture and variety of retail outlets specialising in everything from fishing tackle to designer children's wear, the town has much to offer, why not pop into one of several Scottish gift shops which are brim full of quality products. Have a home made ice cream or a cup of tea and a giant doughnut at Chaplins or visit the small but excellent Country Hamper deli. If you fancy stretching your legs there are a series of marked trails through Anagach Woods and along the Speyside Way. The woods offer a unique habitat for a wide variety of wildlife, including deer, wildcat, capercaillie and red squirrels.

Whilst heading downstream pop into the Spey Valley Smokehouse, just outside Grantown-on-Spey on the A95 Elgin road. The traditional smoking methods used here have been handed down through the generations and these, combined with other specialised techniques, produce the very finest Scottish Smoked Salmon. The glass viewing gallery gives visitors the chance to see the whole process from the arrival of the fresh fish to the packaging of the finished product ready for sale in some of the world's most prestigious outlets. You could always take a short diversion here and take the A939 to Tomintoul and visit the World Famous Whisky Castle, you will be made most welcome and Mike, Cathy and their staff provide informative tastings and expert guidance.

It's not just the whisky and salmon that have made Speyside famous, dedicated local producers of meat, vegetables and soft fruits are world renowned for the quality of their produce and for their guardianship and conservation of the environment. Alistair and Ann McClennan of Balliefurth Farm near the village of Nethy Bridge are prime examples of such people. Alistair won the Scottish Silver Lapwing Award in recognition of his conservation work whilst maintaining a profitable farm. Alistair offers tours around the farm to show how he combines farming and conservation.

Through the wide valley, the river leads you into the most concentrated malt whisky production region in Scotland boasting half of Scotland's distilleries within this small area. Here we have the famous Malt Whisky Trail where well known names stand shoulder to shoulder with less famous brands. Many of the distilleries have visitor centres and guided tours which take you to the heart of the whisky making process whilst providing a potted history of the industry's past. Others offer in-depth tuition into how whisky is made and provide unique tasting experiences.

The malts of Speyside are essentially sweet, few displaying much, if any, peaty character, although there are a few exceptions. On the nose there is a predominance of boiled sweets, even mango and guava, most underlined with a hint of vanilla. These characteristics are born of the normal Speyside practice of maturation in sherry casks and contribute to the creation of some of the most complex and pleasing malts.

The towns of Aberlour, Dufftown and Rothes are at the heart of the Whisky Trail and offer the visitor the chance to while away a few hours in their museums, whisky shops and restaurants. Worthy of a visit is the Aberlour Distillery which still retains its individual charm and the tasting session at the end is one of the best we have attended. Then step back in time as you enter the wonderful Spey Larder in Aberlour. The current owners have maintained the Victorian layout with the original wooden shelves reaching right up to the high ceiling. They offer the finest of Scottish produce, including home baked breads and biscuits and a fantastic cheese and deli centrepiece. They also offer take-away sandwiches and soup. Whilst in Aberlour, stop and have a snack at The Mash Tun Whisky Bar. It is well stocked with real ales and of course whiskies but they also house the only complete Glenfarclas Family Cask Collection available by the glass. Every May the Spirit of Speyside Whisky Festival takes place in and around the towns of Aberlour and Dufftown. The Festival continues to develop the marriage of its world famous malt whiskies with the wide variety of fresh quality produce and the skills of the region's chefs who source and prepare it so skilfully. In 2007, co-author Graham Harvey was chosen unanimously by the competition judges as the worthy first ever Spirit of Speyside Chef of the Year.

The river finally spills out into the Moray Firth at Spey Bay. Originally a fishing village, it is now home to Spey Bay Golf Club and The Whale and Dolphin Conservation Centre housed in the original salmon fishing station and is a great place to end your journey along the River Spey - you might even be lucky enough to see the dolphins.

Speyside is an essential destination for anyone visiting Scotland

Roast Supreme of Guinea Fowl

Black Bottle's underlying sweetness provides a delicious link between the guinea fowl and the sauce.
Guinea Fowl makes a wonderful tasty change from chicken. Here we have used a supreme and have cooked it extremely simply, it really doesn't need a lot of additional flavours or a heavy sauce.

Preheat oven to 220C/Gas 7

▪ Start by making the potato galette. When the galette is in the oven, place the whisky in a dish and lay the guinea fowl, flesh side down on top. Set aside for a few minutes until you are ready to cook it. Now mix the sea salt, rosemary and fennel seeds together. Dry the guinea fowl skin and coat it with the olive oil then sprinkle the salt mixture quite thickly over it.

Reduce oven heat to 200C/Gas 6

▪ Place on a baking tray and roast for about 15-20 minutes, this will depend on the size of the supremes. To check that it is cooked pierce the plumpest part of the breast with a skewer and if the juices run clear, it is cooked.
▪ While it is cooking prepare the sauce and set it aside.
▪ Remove the guinea fowl from the oven and keep warm, allow them to rest for at least 5 minutes.
▪ Add the resting juices to the Whisky Madeira sauce along with the redcurrants and heat up to serve.

To Serve
▪ Place a wedge of potato galette on each plate, cut the supreme in half and place on top and then trickle the sauce around it. Place your chosen vegetables on the plate and serve.

Variation
▪ Serve on a bed of sliced potatoes, sautéed with bacon and onions.

1 Potato Galette (page 117)
4 supremes of Guinea Fowl
20mls Black Bottle Blended Scotch Whisky
olive oil to baste the guinea fowl
1 teaspoon sea salt
1/2 teaspoon dried rosemary, crushed
1/2 teaspoon dried fennel seeds, crushed
Whisky Madeira sauce (page 142)
100g redcurrants, frozen are fine if you can't get fresh
vegetables of your choice

Main Courses

Chicken with Whisky and Wild Mushrooms

Highland Park 12 year old has a delicious malty background and a distinct wood smoke finish that links the wild mushrooms and the chicken through the sauce. You could use only fresh wild mushrooms, but adding the reconstituted dried mushrooms intensifies the flavour and works so well with the whisky.

Serves 4

4 skinless chicken breasts

2 tablespoons plain flour, seasoned with salt and pepper

butter and olive oil for frying

2 shallots, finely chopped

250g chanterelles (or other wild mushrooms)

30g dried wild mushrooms, reconstituted as instructed on the pack, retaining the mushroom water

90mls Highland Park 12 year old Malt Whisky

225mls chicken stock

225mls double cream

1 sprig of fresh thyme or a pinch of dried thyme

■ Toss the chicken breasts in the seasoned flour, dusting off any excess. Heat the butter and oil in a large frying pan and fry the chicken on all sides until golden brown. Now remove the chicken from the pan and set aside.

■ Reduce the heat and gently fry the shallots. Do not brown. Now add the fresh wild mushrooms and cook gently for about 5 minutes. Next return the chicken to the pan and add the reconstituted dried mushrooms with most of the liquid, pour in the whisky, stock, mushroom water, cream and thyme. Bring to a simmer, cover with a lid or with tinfoil and cook gently for 12-15 minutes or until the chicken is just cooked. *(this will depend on the size of the chicken breasts).*

■ Lift the chicken pieces and mushrooms out of the juices and keep warm. Remove the sprig of thyme and boil the juices hard to reduce to thicken. Adjust the seasoning as necessary.

To Serve

■ Place a slice of dauphinoise potatoes (see page 102) or potato galette (page 117) on each plate, lay a chicken breast beside it and coat with the sauce. Alternatively, slice the chicken, place the pieces on top of the potato and pour the sauce around it, as in the photograph. Add fresh vegetables and serve.

Variations

■ You could use chicken tenderloins and keep combined with the sauce to create a homely casserole dish and serve with mashed potatoes and steamed spring greens.

■ As this mixture is also delicious cold, you can use this recipe to make wonderful canapés or a starter. When cold, chop it into smallish pieces and use it to fill either tiny or normal size vol au vents or little short crust pastry cases.

Tea Smoked Duck with Cherry and Cashew Nut Salad

If you have never tried home smoking before you will be surprised by how simple it is. The Earl Grey and the star anise imbue the duck with a delicate oriental flavour and the cashew nuts add a little sweetness and texture to the salad. We have teamed it with cherries, which of course is a classic combination but we have added Jura 10 year old which enhances the delicious fruitiness of the sauce.

Preheat oven to 200C/Gas 6

▪ Line the inside of a heavy roasting tin with tin foil and place the rice, tea leaves, star anise, orange peel and sugar in it. Brush your cooling rack or grill rack with a little oil and place it over the smoking ingredients.

▪ Score the duck skin in a crosshatch pattern with a sharp knife making sure you don't cut through to the meat.

Heat the pan over a moderate heat. Place the roasting tin on the heat on the hob and when it begins to smoke place the duck breasts on the rack. Cover rack and the top of the roasting tin with tin foil, sealing in the edges. Reduce the heat to low to medium and slowly smoke for 12 minutes. I suggest that you open a window and turn on your extraction fan.... Remove the roasting tin from the heat. Remove the duck from the rack, it will now be almost cooked and a brown smoked colour. Heat a frying pan with a little olive oil over a medium heat. Fry the breasts, skin side down, for 3 minutes. Turn the breasts over and cook for about 1 minute. Remove the duck from the pan and allow to rest for 5 minutes. This should result in a medium rare finish depending on the size of the breasts.

▪ While the duck is resting prepare the cherry sauce. Place the stock in a pan and bring to the boil and reduce by a half, add the oil, vinegar, mustard, soy sauce, orange juice, whisky, cherries, the 50mls of reserved cherry syrup plus the juices from the resting duck. Whisk together whilst heating for about 3 minutes. Season carefully with salt and pepper and add a little more whisky to taste if you like. Add the butter and whisk in. Allow to cool.

To Serve (either warm or cold)

▪ Dress the salad leaves with a little cherry sauce and place a handful on each plate. Slice the duck thinly at an angle and place on top of the salad. Sprinkle the nuts over the duck and add a little more sauce as a dressing. Place a few cherries in the dressing and you are ready to serve.

Variation

▪ This dish is also delicious served hot with noodles.

Serves 4

Smoking Mixture

1 tablespoon uncooked rice

5 tablespoons Earl Grey tea leaves

3 star anise

the peel of one orange

1 tablespoon dark soft brown sugar, preferably muscavado

2 large duck breasts

Cherry Sauce

250mls meat or vegetable stock

30mls hazelnut oil

30mls white wine vinegar

1 teaspoon Dijon mustard

15mls soy sauce

10mls fresh orange juice

15mls Jura 10 year old Malt Whisky

24 cherries drained from a bottle or tin of cherries in syrup. Reserve 50mls of the syrup

salt and freshly ground black pepper

25g unsalted butter

Garnish

50g chopped cashew nuts (or pistachios, hazelnuts, macadamia nuts or pecans)

You will need a heavy roasting tin and a cooling or grill rack which fits inside it.

Main Courses

Highland Pheasant Casserole

Royal Lochnagar 12 year old's woody, earthy background backs up the wild mushroom flavours in this hearty one pot dish. The sauce is full of incredible big flavours but the long slow cooking is the real secret of this delicious casserole, sometimes pheasant can be a bit tough, but not here....

Preheat oven to 150C/Gas 2

■ Start by making stock from the giblets of the pheasant, if you have them, by simmering for about an hour with a carrot, a small onion, a stick of celery, ½ a leek, a large bay leaf and 4 black peppercorns and 1 litre water. Strain before using. Whilst the stock is cooking, heat the olive oil in a casserole dish on the hob and add the pheasant joints, brown them all over in the oil and set aside.

■ Fry the bacon in the casserole, add all the chopped vegetables, stir in and cook for about 3 minutes then add the flour and stir in thoroughly. Add the soaked mushrooms to the casserole then the pheasant, the whisky, stock, cider, Worcestershire Sauce, balsamic vinegar, and the liquid from the dried mushrooms. Put on the lid or cover tightly with tin foil and cook very slowly in the oven for 2-3 hours until the meat is tender.

■ Next, sauté the sliced wild mushrooms with the butter and garlic for 2 or 3 minutes. Remove the casserole from the oven and add the mushrooms to the sauce along with the apples and apple and rosehip jelly. Stir in and return to the oven for 15 minutes to cook the apples and combine the flavours.

■ Lift the joints out of the pan, place on a plate and keep warm. Place the casserole back on the hob on a low heat, to reduce to a little. Add salt and pepper to taste and stir in the fresh herbs, adding a little more whisky to taste if desired.

To Serve
■ Garnish with chopped parsley and serve with new potatoes or Dijon mustard mash.

Serves 4

2 pheasants with giblets if possible ask your butcher to joint the birds for you

3 tablespoons olive oil

225g smoked bacon chopped

1 large onion, chopped

2 sticks celery, sliced

4 cloves of garlic peeled and crushed

2 carrots, sliced

100g swede (neep), peeled and chopped

1 tablespoon plain flour

25g dried wild mushrooms, reconstitute them as directed, drain and reserve the strained liquid

60mls Royal Lochnagar 12 year old Malt Whisky

300ml giblet or chicken stock

300ml cider

1 tablespoon Worcestershire sauce

1 tablespoon Balsamic Vinegar

100g fresh wild mushrooms, chanterelles are lovely

a little unsalted butter

1 plump clove of garlic, crushed

2 cooking apples, peeled, cored and cut into chunks

2 tablespoons Apple and Rosehip Jelly (page 146) or a bought Apple Jelly

1 tablespoon fresh parsley, chopped

1 tablespoon fresh thyme, the leaves stripped off the stems

salt and freshly ground black pepper

Garnish
fresh flat leaf parsley, chopped

Tullibardine™ laced Mustard and Honey Glazed Chicken

Tullibardine Single Malt Whisky's fruity flavour and hints of vanilla and orange are a perfect marriage with the sweetness of the honey and the spicy mustard.
This simple dish will wow your family but is equally at home at a dinner party.

Serves 4

Preheat Oven to180C/Gas 4

◾ First season the chicken breasts and fry them until browned on both sides and then place them in a roasting tin.

◾ Next, deglaze the frying pan with the chicken stock and whisky and reduce it by half, add the honey, balsamic vinegar and wholegrain mustard, mix well and bring back to a simmer. Pour most of it over the chicken, reserving some for a dressing when you serve it.

◾ Roast in the oven for about 10-15 minutes or until the chicken is cooked but check occasionally to ensure it is not getting too brown. If it is, cover the dish with tinfoil.

To test to see if the chicken is cooked, pierce a plump piece of chicken with a skewer and if the juices run clear, it is cooked.

4 skinless chicken breasts
salt and freshly ground black pepper
30mls chicken stock
30mls Tullibardine Single Malt Whisky
100g honey
2 teaspoon balsamic vinegar
50g wholegrain mustard
1 ripe avocado, sliced
a few slices of ripe melon

To Serve

◾ Cut the chicken into slices and drizzle the remaining whisky, mustard and honey glaze on top then serve with mixed salad leaves, slices of avocado and melon with thinly sliced red onion. *Lovely.....*

Variation

◾ Leave the breast whole and glaze it with the mustard and honey sauce and serve with roasted potatoes and fresh vegetables.

Scottish Breakfast Salad

This robust salad needs a robust whisky to complement the spicy black pudding and the smoky spicy Oban 14 year old is well up to the task.

This is a delicious Scottish twist on the French classic Salade aux Lardons. The Oban dressing is wonderful and I'm sure that it will become a firm favourite. It also works well with chicken and just try it with smoked mackerel, lovely!

■ Start by making the dressing. Place all the ingredients in a jam jar (or other container) with a lid and shake to mix and emulsify then set aside. Shake again before use.

■ Make the croutons, cut the bread into cubes and fry in a little oil until browned and crispy, set aside. Take care not to burn them!

■ Cut the bacon into pieces and place into a pre-heated frying pan, with a small amount of oil and fry until crisp, remove and keep warm. Cut the black pudding and haggis into cubes and cook in a frying pan or in a hot oven until crisp.

■ Meanwhile bring a pan of water and 1 tablespoon white wine vinegar to the boil, reduce the heat to a simmer and break the eggs carefully into the water then simmer gently for about 1 minute. Remove from the heat and allow to stand for another minute or until the eggs are set. When the eggs are cooked, remove them with a slotted spoon draining on to a paper towel.

■ Wash the salad leaves, dry and quickly toss them in a little salad dressing. Now place a pile of the dressed leaves on the centre of each plate. Place the bacon, black pudding, croutons and haggis decoratively on the salad leaves and top with a poached egg. Season the eggs with salt and freshly ground black pepper and serve immediately.

Serves 4

Oban™ Dressing
15mls Oban 14 year old Malt Whisky
1 tablespoon wholegrain mustard
1 tablespoon balsamic vinegar
pinch of sugar
90mls olive oil
salt and pepper

The Breakfast
2 slices of white bread
a little oil for frying
8 rashers of your favourite butcher's bacon
150g black pudding
150g haggis
4 large free range eggs
1 tablespoon white wine vinegar
250g mixed leaves
salt and freshly ground black pepper

Parmesan Pork Escalopes

The 10 year old Isle of Jura sweetness and delicate malt layer, combined with its overall saltiness are great background notes for the sauce for this dish. It takes Graham back to when he lived in Germany and pork schnitzels were one of his favourite takeaway meals.
This is a lovely dish with Italian roots, it is perfect for dinner but it is so quick it would make a wonderful lunch. The tasty crisp breadcrumb coating contrasts beautifully with the moist pork inside and the chunky whisky and tomato sauce is the perfect partner.

Preheat oven to 200C/Gas 6

■ Beat the egg with a little water in a shallow dish. Combine the grated Parmesan and breadcrumbs with oregano, garlic salt and black pepper in another shallow dish. Dip the pork in the egg and then in the crumb mixture to coat. Place on a tray, layer with cling film, cover and place in the fridge while you cook the tomato sauce.

■ Heat about 1 tablespoon of olive oil in a saucepan over a medium heat. Fry the onion and garlic gently until soft, about 7 minutes. Add the chopped tomatoes and balsamic vinegar with the whisky and season with oregano, salt and pepper. Reduce the heat to low, cover and simmer on a low heat for 20 minutes, stirring occasionally. Taste and add seasoning and a little more whisky to taste.

■ Heat a large frying pan with a little olive oil over medium heat. Fry the pork for about 2 minutes on each side until nicely browned. Drain on paper towels, then place on a baking tray, top each escalope with a slice of mozzarella and put in the oven until the mozzarella begins to melt. Meanwhile place a spoonful of tomato sauce on each plate and top with an escalope and garnish with a sprig of basil.

To Serve

■ This can be served with pasta dressed with chopped fresh parsley, a fondant potato or new potatoes and a side salad or fresh vegetables. Offer freshly grated Parmesan separately.

Pork Escalope
1 egg
125g freshly grated Parmesan cheese
125g dry fresh breadcrumbs
pinch dried oregano
$^1/_2$ teaspoon garlic salt
freshly ground black pepper
4 escalopes of pork, pounded to 6mm/ $^1/_4$ inch thickness
olive oil

Whisky and Tomato Sauce
olive oil for frying
1 medium onion, chopped finely
2 plump cloves of garlic, crushed
400g canned chopped tomatoes
2 teaspoons balsamic vinegar
30-50mls Jura 10 year old Malt Whisky, to taste
1 teaspoon dried oregano
salt and freshly ground black pepper

Topping
225g buffalo mozzarella cheese, sliced
freshly grated Parmesan cheese

Roast Belly Pork with Crackling, Apples and Onions

The complexity of Cragganmore 12 year old, specifically its honey, cooked fruits and dried apricot notes, lend a very pleasing note to the gravy for this delicious pork dish.

This is a wonderful recipe: the crackling is perfect every time and because it is slow cooked the meat is so tender it just melts in the mouth. We have cut it into individual portions so you don't have the problem of slicing the joint through the crackling. It does take a few hours to achieve this but it is well worth waiting for. Pork belly is an inexpensive cut of meat which when cooked in this way a lot of the fat is rendered out and you then have a very special dish which will look like something from a top restaurant (as indeed it is!)

Preheat oven to 220C/Gas 7

■ Start by cutting the onions into thick slices and then core and cut the apples into thick rings. Place the onion slices in a deep sided roasting tin and apples on top and season with a little salt and freshly ground black pepper. Set aside.

■ Lay the piece of pork, skin side up on your chopping board and cut into 6 pieces. You will notice that one end of the pork has less meat than the other, so cut the pieces from that end a little larger. Now using a sharp knife slice into the fat creating several lines on each piece of pork, be careful not to cut all the way through to the meat or the juices will come out and your meat will be dry. All you are doing is helping the fat to render out and beginning the process of creating wonderful crackling. Now massage quite a lot of salt into the skin.

■ Now lay each piece of pork on top of the onion and apple slices, this raises the pork out of the fat and roasting juices whilst it is cooking and it also protects the onion and apple from burning. Next place the roasting tin on the top shelf of your oven and allow to cook for about 45 minutes or until the crackling starts to crisp. You are not waiting for all of the crackling to bubble up and crisp, just until it starts, this may take an hour depending on your oven, but do not allow it to burn and do not allow the onion and apple to dry out and burn. If you are worried about it move to the next step.

■ Now turn the oven down to 160C/Gas 3, move the roasting tin to the bottom shelf and pour the white wine and whisky around the pork then cook for a further 2 hours approximately until all the crackling has "crackled". Check on the progress of the pork after the first hour but do not be tempted to baste, or you will ruin the crackling. Sometimes you have to turn the tray or the individual pork pieces around to facilitate even cooking of the crackling.

■ Meanwhile make the **röstis**. Begin by parboiling the potatoes for about 10minutes, this will enable the röstis to cook more quickly. Allow the potatoes to cool until you are able to handle them. Remove the skins and grate the potatoes either with a hand grater or with the grater of your food processor.

Serves 6

2 large onions

3 eating apples

salt and freshly ground black pepper

1 pork belly, they are usually around 1.5kg. (ask your butcher to remove the rib bones and leave the skin on)

500mls dry white wine

50mls Cragganmore 12 year old Malt Whisky

Rosti

500g baking potatoes

1 tablespoon cornflour

2 teaspoons salt

3 sage leaves, finely chopped

You will need a sharp knife to score the skin unless you ask your butcher to do it for you.

Roast Belly Pork with Crackling, Apples and Onions (continued)

Put the grated potato into a large bowl and mix the cornflour, chopped sage and salt thoroughly through them. Place the oil in a large frying pan and put the oiled pastry cutters or egg rings in the pan, pack in the potato mixture and press down firmly. Remove the rings and cook for about 2 or 3 minutes (this will depend on how thick you have made them) on each side at a moderate heat until they are golden brown and crisp on the outside and cooked in the middle. Don't try to cook them all at once, you need room in the frying pan to turn them and you possibly won't have enough rings. Remove the röstis from the pan and repeat until you have made 6. Set them aside and keep warm until you are ready to serve. *Röstis can be made well in advance and reheated just before serving.*

Now back to the pork. Remove the roasting tray from the oven, take the pork out and if any have not "crackled" as much as you would like, pop the individual pieces on a small tray back in the oven for a few minutes. Remove the onion and apple and set aside, keeping warm. Keep the pork pieces warm while they rest for about 10 minutes.

Now empty the pan juices into a bowl and allow to cool, so that the fat will rise to the top, remove as much of it as you can and then put the liquid in a saucepan with the juices from the resting pork and from the apples and onion. This will be your gravy. All you have to do is simply reduce it by about half over a high heat, add seasoning and a little more whisky to taste and you are ready to serve. *You can prepare to this stage a day or two in advance, cover well and refrigerate until you are ready to serve. The pork heats up beautifully in the oven at a high heat and if there are gaps in your crackling, you can add a little salt to the soft bits before it goes in the oven.*

To Serve

Using a sharp knife separate the crackling from the pork and replace it back on top, this will make it easier for your guests to eat. Put a rösti on each plate, place one serving of onion and apple on each and then top each with the roast pork and crackling. Add your chosen fresh vegetables, pour sauce around and serve with pride....

Variations

Instead of serving the pork on a rösti it is also lovely served with kailkenny mash (mashed potato with cooked cabbage and a little double cream mixed through it).

You can also make an apple rösti by putting a layer of cooked apple in the centre of each rösti when you are making it.

Peppered Pork Fillet

Royal Lochnagar 12 year old has woody, nutty undertones and a caramel and liquorice background that give this dish a rich depth of flavour.
Very easy but oh so tasty... Suitable for a family meal or for a dinner party.

Serves 4

Preheat oven to 200C/Gas 6

To start, roll the pork fillets in the cracked peppercorns, then melt the butter with the olive oil in large frying pan or wok, add the pork and brown on all sides. Remove from the pan and place on an ovenproof tray and cook into the oven for 10-12 minutes. Remove from the oven and keeping the pork warm, allow it to rest for 5 minutes before serving.

Meanwhile, add the carrots to the pan and stir fry for 3-5 minutes. Add the onions, pepper, chilli, mushrooms, mangetout peas and garlic and cook for a few minutes until the vegetables are tender but still crisp. Now add the whisky, lemon juice and cream and stir in. Check the seasoning adding more whisky to taste if required. Add any juices from the resting pork to the mixture.

Now divide the creamy vegetable mixture between 4 plates, slice each fillet into 3 and arrange on top of the vegetables.

To Serve

Sprinkle with parsley and serve with noodles, plain boiled rice, mashed or new potatoes.

2 pork fillets, trimmed of all fat and cut into 4 portions

2 teaspoons cracked black peppercorns

25g butter and a little olive oil for frying

300g carrots, cut into matchsticks

1 large onion, chopped

1 small red pepper, seeded and cut into strips

1/2 teaspoon red chilli, deseeded and finely chopped

125g mushrooms, sliced

8 mangetout peas, cut on the diagonal and sliced thinly

1 clove garlic, crushed

75mls Royal Lochnagar 12 year old Malt Whisky

juice of 1/2 lemon

175mls double cream

salt and freshly ground black pepper

Garnish
fresh flat leaf parsley, finely chopped

Seared Lambs Liver

on sweet potato griddle cakes with apples and pink peppercorn sauce

The spicy background notes of Glenfarclas 15 year old create a very pleasing underlying layer of flavour to this delightful combination.

This is a beautiful dish with wonderful complementing flavours. Our customers love it and I hope you will too. We have created this as a main course dish but it would make a most unusual starter.

Serves 4

■ Make the Pink Peppercorn Sauce first. Pour the red wine and whisky into a pan and reduce by about a half, add the stock and reduce again by about one third, pour in the cream and bring back to the boil and reduce to desired consistency. Season with salt and pepper and add the pink peppercorns and set aside.

■ Next peel and chop the sweet potato and boil until tender, drain and return to the hot pan and allow to dry out, then mash. Meanwhile grate the potatoes and stir into the mash. Season with salt and pepper and add the flour. Stir in to combine well. Beat the egg and stir it into the mixture, adding enough milk to make a batter that will drop easily from a spoon. Now heat a frying pan to moderately hot add a little olive oil and drop tablespoonfuls into greased rings and cook for 4-5 minutes on each side. They are ready to turn when bubbles come through the surface. Keep warm.

■ Prepare the liver by removing the skin and any big tubes, cut into medium thick slices and set aside to marinate in 15mls whisky for 20 minutes. The remaining marinade can be added to the peppercorn sauce. Dry and season with black pepper. Heat a frying pan with a little olive oil and fry the liver quickly for about 1 minute on each side. Turn the heat down and cook for another minute if necessary, the liver should still be pink but not red. Remove from the heat to rest but keep warm, add any juices to the peppercorn sauce.

■ Fry or grill the bacon and the slices of black pudding until crisp. Set aside and keep warm. Meanwhile core the apples, no need to peel them, cut in half and then into slices. Fry them in a little olive oil until they start to caramelise.

To Serve

■ Place a griddle cake on each plate, top with a slice of black pudding and a few pieces of apple, now some pieces of liver and then finish with apple. Arrange the liver and the bacon leaning on the stack or on top, it depends on the size of the slices of liver. Be creative! Now surround the stacks with the warmed up peppercorn sauce. *And doesn't that look good! Tastes good too!*

Pink Peppercorn Sauce
200mls red wine
25mls Glenfarclas 15 year old Malt Whisky
300mls good beef stock
50mls double cream
1 tablespoon pink peppercorns in brine (if you can't find them, use green)

Sweet Potato Griddle Cakes
200g sweet potato
200g potatoes
salt and freshly ground black pepper
125g self raising flour
1 large free range egg
milk to mix
500g lambs liver
15mls Glenfarclas 15 year old Malt Whisky
olive oil
4 slices black pudding
4 rashers middle bacon
2 dessert apples

You will need 4 mousse rings 8cm diameter x 4cm high.

Dundee Lamb Chops with Jura™ Malt Whisky Sauce

Jura has a delicate nose and salty, nutty finish that balance the strong flavours of this marinade, providing a subtle edge to the dish.

Dundee has long been associated with marmalade so that now whenever marmalade is added to a recipe it immediately gets entitled "Dundee". Here the dish is enhanced even further with the addition of Jura 10 year old. As you will find, whisky and oranges go very well together.

Serves 4

8 best end of lamb chops

Preheat oven to 200C/Gas 6

▪ Mix together all of the marinade ingredients in a bowl and add the chops, turning them in the marinade. Set aside for no longer than 15 minutes.

▪ Heat a large frying pan and add the chops fat side down, brown the fat then turn the chops and sear on all sides. Put the chops in an ovenproof dish or tray and place it on the top shelf of the oven for 5-10 minutes, depending on how well done you like your lamb chops.

▪ Meanwhile add the marinade to the pan that the chops were cooked in, heat and stir in the marmalade, check the seasoning, adding salt and pepper or more whisky to taste.

▪ Remove the chops from the oven and keep warm while you leave them to rest for about 5 minutes.

▪ Finally add the juices from the chops to the sauce pan, heat and then stir in a knob of butter just before you serve it. This will help to thicken the sauce and make it glossy. Heat carefully, but if it splits don't worry, just add a little cold stock and whisk it in.

Marinade
1 tablespoon olive oil
1 teaspoon ground allspice
1 plump clove of garlic, crushed
20mls heather honey
salt and freshly ground black pepper
50mls white wine vinegar
75mls stock (lamb or vegetable)
60mls Jura 10 year old Malt Whisky
2 teaspoons orange marmalade
a large knob of butter

Garnish
8 thin slices orange

To Serve

▪ Place the chops leaning against each other in the centre of the plate and garnish with the slices of orange. Spoon the sauce around the chops and serve with boiled new potatoes and fresh vegetables.

Steak and Kidney Pie

Here we have everyone's favourite, a good old fashioned Steak Pie but this time the recipe contains a bottle of beer and more importantly, a whisky chaser. The beer brings a richness and depth of flavour to the gravy and the Knockando 12 year old pumps up the volume. Rough Puff Pastry is my favourite for a meat pie, it has the crispness of short crust without the empty flakiness of puff pastry and it's not difficult to make.

■ For the pastry, sieve the flour and salt into a bowl. Now grate the frozen butter coarsely into the flour, dipping it in the flour as necessary, also make sure you peel the wrapping back so that it does not get grated too.... Cut the butter into the flour with a knife adding enough lemon juice and water to form a dough. There should still be bits of butter showing in the dough. On a floured surface, roll the dough into a rectangle just under 1cm thick. Fold the bottom third up and the top third down and seal the open edges with a rolling pin. Give the pastry half a turn so that the folds are at the sides. Roll out. Repeat 4 times taking care not to burst the air bubbles that will rise. Place in a polythene bag or wrap in cling film and refrigerate for thirty minutes to one hour to rest and firm up - this is very important. Ideally, if you have the time, the dough should also be placed in a polythene bag in the fridge for 15 minutes between rollings. Remove from the fridge about 30 minutes before you need it to allow it to return to room temperature before the final rolling.

■ Heat a large lidded pan and add half of the vegetable oil and butter then cook the chopped onion gently for 7 minutes until soft. Add the mushrooms to the pan and cook for about 2 minutes, remove to a bowl and set aside. Place the seasoned flour in a large polythene bag, add the steak and toss around in the flour until lightly coated. Add the remaining oil and butter to the pan, heat and cook the steak and kidney until no longer pink, adding more oil as necessary. Put the onions and mushrooms back in the pan, stir in and add the remaining ingredients and bring to the boil, stirring well. Cover and cook gently for 1½ hours, stirring occasionally until the meat is tender. Remove the bay leaves and if the gravy is not thick enough add little bits of beurre manié and mix in, continuing to simmer until it reaches the thickness you like. Check the seasoning and set aside to cool.

Serves 6

Rough Puff Pastry
(worth making yourself, but a ready rolled butter puff pastry, can be substituted)
330g plain flour
1 large pinch salt
250g butter, in its wrapping paper or tinfoil. Freeze for 45 minutes.
8 tablespoon iced water
1 teaspoon lemon juice
1 beaten egg, to glaze

Pie filling
50mls vegetable oil
50g butter
1 large onion, peeled and roughly chopped
225g field mushrooms, wiped clean and cut into chunks
50g plain flour, seasoned with salt and freshly ground black pepper
1 kg round steak, (shoulder steak or rump) cut into chunks
250g ox kidney, the white core removed and the kidney cut into bite sized pieces
1 bottle ale, 330mls
300mls good beef stock
60mls Knockando 12 year old Malt Whisky
50mls Worcestershire sauce
1 teaspoon tomato purée
1 level teaspoon dried thyme
2 bay leaves
salt and lots of freshly ground black pepper

50g plain flour mixed with 50g butter to a paste for thickening the gravy. (beurre manié)

Preheat the oven to 200C/Gas 6

You will need a 1.2 litre / 2 pint pie dish.

■ Roll out the pastry on a floured surface to just over ½ cm thick and 3cm wider than your pie dish. Cut out the lid so it is slightly bigger than the dish. Cut a strip of pastry to fit the rim of the pie dish.
■ Place a pie funnel or an egg cup in the centre of the pie dish and pour the filling around it, if there is too much, set some of the gravy aside to serve separately when the pie is cooked. Brush the rim of the pie dish with water, lay the pastry strip on top, seal and brush it with egg. Now place the lid on top, seal the edges, knock them up with a knife and flute the edge. Cut a slit in the lid over the pie funnel, brush with the egg (but not the edges or they won't rise) and decorate with the excess pastry also brushed with egg. Bake in the oven for 15 to 20 minutes until golden brown then allow it to cool for a few minutes before serving.

Main Courses

The Ultimate Steak Burger

Jura is a very versatile whisky and one you should consider keeping in the store cupboard, it links this really tasty burger and the tomato sauce.

These are fantastic burgers, tastier, juicier and much healthier than the bought versions. Here we have served them with potato röstis, a chunky whisky and tomato sauce and a side salad.

Serves 4

olive oil for frying
2 shallots, chopped
400g minced steak
3 large gherkins, chopped
1 plump clove of garlic, chopped
15mls double cream
2 teaspoons tomato puree
1/2 teaspoon Dijon mustard
1 teaspoon fresh flat leaf parsley, chopped
1 teaspoon of Worcestershire sauce
15-30mls Jura 10 year old Malt Whisky
1 egg yolk
salt and freshly ground black pepper

■ Gently fry the shallots in a little olive oil until softened, then place with all the other ingredients into the food processor and whizz until well blended. Season with plenty of salt and pepper.

■ If you don't have a food processor, chop the shallots finely and cook as above. Chop the gherkins and garlic very finely then mix all ingredients thoroughly in a bowl, this is easiest with your hands.

■ With wet hands, divide the mixture into 4 equal sized pieces and shape into burgers. Place on a plate and refrigerate for 30 minutes. Fry, barbecue or grill using a moderately high heat for 5-6 minutes on each side or until the burger is cooked through.

■ While the burger is chilling in the fridge, make the röstis and keep warm. Make the Whisky and Tomato Sauce and set aside then finally, whilst the burgers are cooking, heat the vegetable oil in a frying pan and cook the onion slices until caramelised and golden brown. If you add a pinch of sugar it will help them to caramelise.

Potato Rösti
see page 80

Whisky and Tomato Sauce
see page 78

Crispy fried Onions
1 large onion, thinly sliced
vegetable oil

To Serve

■ Place a rösti in the centre of each plate and top with the burger with a spoonful of onions on top. Surround with the whisky and tomato sauce and serve with a fresh mixed salad.

Variation

■ Whisky Madeira Sauce is also a wonderful accompaniment to this posh burger (see page 142).

Main Courses

Black Bottle Beef Olives

Black Bottle Blended Scotch Whisky, the blend that contains seven Islay malts has a full rich palate, with a slightly honeyed sweetness and a distinctive yet pleasing smoky flavour which prevails throughout the marinated beef as well as the stuffing. I have written this recipe for my sister Joyce who loves oatmeal and beef olives. This traditional Scottish dish which has been enjoyed here since the 1600's is brought up to date with the wonderful flavour of Black Bottle . The Olives are stuffed with a lightly spiced oatmeal mixture which I think complements the dish perfectly. The braised vegetables are in a delicious flavoursome sauce. This is comfort food which would also not be out of place as part of a posh evening meal.

Preheat oven to 150C/Gas 2

◾ Place the strips of steak in a bowl with the whisky and set aside to marinate until you have prepared the stuffing and the vegetables.

◾ Prepare the stuffing by frying the onion gently in the olive oil for a few minutes until softened. Add it to a bowl with all the other ingredients and stir in, adding sufficient milk to bind the mixture together. Set aside.

◾ Prepare the vegetables as above and set aside.

◾ Lay out the 8 slices of steak, season and spread with a little Dijon mustard. Now lay a spoonful of stuffing across the narrow end of each steak, dividing the stuffing equally between them. Firmly roll up and secure with a cocktail stick or with fine butchers string.

◾ Heat 25ml olive oil in a pan and brown the beef olives on all sides, this will add additional flavour, then remove them and set them aside. Into the same pan, add all of the root vegetables from the braising list and lightly brown them. Remove the vegetables to a roasting tin or large casserole big enough to hold the beef olives as well. Next, deglaze the pan with the red wine and whisky and reduce by half, this will also cook out the alcohol. Add the tomato purée, balsamic vinegar, thyme and beef stock, bring back to the boil and cook for a few minutes to reduce by about a half again. Season with salt and pepper.

◾ Place the olives on top of the vegetables and pour over the reduced sauce. Cover with a lid or tin foil and cook in the oven for about 2½ hours, checking every ½ hour to ensure that the sauce does not dry out. Add more stock as necessary.

To Serve

◾ Place a spoonful of mashed potato flavoured with Dijon mustard in the centre of each plate. Top with the beef olives, (don't forget to remove the string or cocktail stick!) surround with the braised vegetables and then coat the beef olives with the sauce. Garnish with a sprig of parsley. *Wonderful on a cold wintry day.*

Serves 4

800g Topside, Rump or Round Steak, very thinly sliced. Tell your butcher that you want to make beef olives and he will cut the strips for you. You will need 8 strips, approximately 25cm long and 5cm wide weighing about 100g each
30mls Black Bottle Blended Scotch Whisky
salt and freshly ground black pepper
1 teaspoon Dijon Mustard

Stuffing
1 small onion, chopped finely
olive oil, to fry the onion
60g medium oatmeal
25g fresh breadcrumbs
25g chopped suet (or butter substitute or melted butter)
1 clove of garlic, crushed
½ teaspoon red chilli, deseeded and chopped finely
30mls Black Bottle Blended Scotch Whisky
1 teaspoon fresh flat leaf parsley, finely chopped
salt and freshly ground black pepper
a little milk to bind

Vegetables and Sauce for Braising
1 tablespoon olive oil
12 shallots, peeled and left whole or if very large divided into cloves
2 medium/large carrots, cut into thick slices
1 small neep (swede), cut into chunky pieces, similar in size to the carrots
2 sticks celery, cleaned and cut into chunky pieces
200mls red wine
50mls Black Bottle Blended Scotch Whisky
25g tomato purée
25mls balsamic vinegar
1 pinch of thyme
1 litre beef stock
salt and freshly ground black pepper

Garnish
fresh flat leaf parsley

You will need cocktail sticks or fine butchers string and a large casserole dish or roasting tin.

Auchentoshan® Stroganoff

The mellowness of the Auchentoshan Three Wood Malt Whisky and its nutty spicy overtones provides a subtle contrast to the slight sharpness of the mustard and the crème fraîche in this delicious creamy but sharp dish.
This recipe makes a wonderful dinner party main course but is also a lovely family meal which will have them clamouring for seconds.....

■ Melt the butter with the olive oil in large frying pan until hot, add the paprika, chopped onion and garlic and cook gently until soft but not brown, this will take about 10 minutes. Add the mushrooms and cook for about 3 minutes then remove from the pan and set aside.

■ Add a little oil to the pan and heat then add half of the steak and cook quickly for about 1 minute, turning until the steak is browned but not fully cooked. Season with salt and black pepper. Remove from the pan and keep warm. Now repeat with the remaining steak. If you cook all of the steak at once the meat will boil instead of browning and it will become tough.

■ Return the onion mushroom mixture to the now empty pan and add the remaining ingredients except the parsley, gherkins and crème fraîche. Bring to the boil and simmer until the sauce thickens, check the seasoning, adding more black pepper and whisky to taste.

■ When you are ready to serve, return the steak, parsley, gherkins and crème fraîche to the pan stir in and warm through for no more than 2 minutes.

To Serve
■ Top with a spoonful of crème fraîche and sprinkle with the remaining chopped parsley and sliced gherkins then serve with boiled rice or mashed potatoes. *Amazing!*

Variations
■ Use Pork strips or more excitingly, try Venison loin cut into strips instead of Steak or for a delicious meat free alternative use Mushrooms, either cultivated, field or mixed wild mushrooms, all equally wonderful. If you decide to try this recipe with venison I can recommend using wild mushrooms with it. *Delicious!*

Serves 4

25g butter and a little olive oil for frying

2 tablespoons paprika

1 large onion, chopped finely

2 plump cloves of garlic, crushed

225g mushrooms, chestnut mushrooms are excellent, leave whole if small, otherwise cut into quarters

700g fillet, sirloin or rump steak, cut into strips

2 teaspoons Dijon mustard

75mls Auchentoshan Three Wood Malt Whisky

2 shakes of Worcestershire Sauce

juice of 1 lemon

salt and freshly ground black pepper

1 tablespoon fresh flat leaf parsley, chopped

300mls crème fraîche or sour cream (you could use double cream plus 2 teaspoons of lemon juice

3 pickled gherkins, thinly sliced

Garnish

100mls crème fraîche

1 tablespoon fresh flat leaf parsley, chopped

2 pickled gherkins, thinly sliced

Scotch Bœuf en Croûte

The overall subtlety of the 12 year old Knockando and the elegance of its peppery finish elevate this already impressive dish to a new level.
This wonderfully glamorous dish is perfect for a dinner party because you can do so much preparation well ahead of the arrival of your guests.

Preheat oven to 220C/Gas 7

Start this dish 3 or 4 hours ahead of serving time.
■ Start by trimming the fillet free of any fat, brush with some of the whisky and set aside for an hour.
Heat the butter and olive oil in a large pan until very hot and brown the joint on all sides, and then roast the beef on a rack in the oven for about 15 minutes until part cooked. Remove the beef from oven and set aside until cold. Reserve any juices from the fillet for the sauce.*
■ Gently fry the shallots and mushrooms in the pan the meat was browned in, adding a little butter if necessary, season with the remaining whisky, salt and black pepper and stir in the thyme and parsley. Allow this mixture to cool until you are ready to complete the dish.

You can prepare up to this point as much as 24 hours in advance, but the beef must be brought to room temperature before wrapping in pastry and cooking or the meat will not cook through in the cooking times given.

■ About 45 minutes before you want to serve the beef, heat the oven to 220C/Gas 7 and begin by rolling out the pastry into a rectangle slightly longer than the joint and wide enough to cover the beef and have sufficient to tuck in and seal. Spread the mushroom mixture in the centre of the pastry and place the beef on top and season lightly with salt and pepper. Cut out 4 squares from each corner of the pastry and set them aside. Brush the edges of the pastry rectangle with beaten egg and wrap them over the beef. *(make sure you don't have too much double thickness because the pastry on the bottom won't cook in time)* Turn the beef parcel over so that the sealed edges are on the bottom. Transfer to a lightly oiled baking sheet and brush with the egg glaze, decorate with the pastry trimmings and glaze them as well. Bake for about 30 minutes until golden brown. *You can test to see if the meat is cooked with a meat thermometer or failing that you can insert a metal skewer into the beef and if it comes out cold it is not cooked, if it is warm it is rare and if it is hot it is well done.*
■ Meanwhile make the sauce. Place the stock in a pan, bring it to the boil then reduce it by a half, add the red wine and reduce again by about a quarter, now add the remaining ingredients, bring back to the boil and check the seasoning.

To Serve
■ Cut the Croûte into thick slices, drizzle some of that glorious sauce around and serve with buttered parsley potatoes and vegetables. *Absolutely wonderful!*

1kg beef fillet
30mls Knockando 12 year old Malt Whisky
butter and olive oil for browning the beef

Mushroom Filling
125g mushrooms, finely chopped
2-3 shallots, finely chopped
salt and freshly ground black pepper
1 large sprig of thyme, with the leaves stripped off the stems (or 1 large pinch of dried thyme)
1 tablespoon fresh flat leaf parsley, finely chopped
350g puff pastry (shop bought is fine, but look for the one made with butter
1 egg, beaten, to glaze pastry

Whisky Sauce
500mls beef stock
200mls red wine
20mls Knockando 12 year old Malt Whisky
juices from the rested fillet*
1 teaspoon redcurrant jelly
1 teaspoon mushroom ketchup
salt and freshly ground black pepper

Main Courses

Venison Steaks with Wild Mushrooms

Cragganmore 12 year old's complexity lends itself to many dishes, here it provides a subtle background layer to this luscious venison dish.

Venison is low in fat and deserves to be on the nation's tables more often. If you cook the steaks quickly as in this dish and allow them to rest, they are meltingly tender. You can use fresh or dried mushrooms or a combination, whichever you choose will taste wonderful, just different. The wild mushrooms have a stronger flavour and will make the sauce darker and richer. I always think that if ingredients grow or live together naturally then they are a good match in a cooked dish and here we have the rich combination of red deer, wild mushrooms, juniper berries, thyme and Scotch Whisky.... and they all work extremely well together.

Serves 4

■ To start, coat the venison steaks in olive oil and a few grinds of black pepper. Now, in a hot frying pan quickly sear the steaks on both sides then cook until medium rare. The meat should still feel slightly soft. Season the steaks with a little salt, remove them from pan and allow them to rest, keeping them warm.

■ Whilst the steaks are cooking, fry the shallots gently in the butter and oil and when almost cooked add the mushrooms, cook them for a few minutes then add the redcurrant jelly, whisky, crushed juniper berries, redcurrants, cream, thyme and seasoning and heat through. *(if you have used dried mushrooms you can add some or all of the rehydrating liquid.)* Add any juices from the resting steaks.

■ Finally check the seasoning; it may need more black pepper.

To Serve
■ Remove the thyme sprig and pour a portion of the sauce on to each plate and place a steak on top, alternatively, cut each steak into slices at an angle and place on top of sauce.

■ Garnish with chopped parsley.

■ Serve with mashed potatoes topped with a little steamed cabbage and a floret of steamed broccoli for each serving.

Variations
■ The venison is also delicious served on top of a potato rösti *(see recipe on page 80)* topped with lightly cooked spring greens or spinach with the sauce poured on the plate around the rösti.

4 x 175g venison steaks

olive oil for coating steaks

freshly ground black pepper

25g butter and olive oil for frying shallots

8 shallots, peeled and divided into their cloves if they are large

125g wild mushrooms (available in most supermarkets, or use dried and follow instructions on pack)

1 tablespoon redcurrant jelly

50ml Cragganmore 12yr old Malt Whisky

10 crushed juniper berries

120g redcurrants, frozen are fine

100ml double cream

sprig of fresh thyme (or 2 large pinches of dried thyme)

salt and lots of freshly ground black pepper

Garnish

fresh flat leaf parsley, finely chopped

Main Courses

Roast Salmon with Aberlour and Orange Jus

Served with Dauphinoise Potatoes and baby Asparagus, garnished with nuggets of Black Pudding

Aberlour 16 year old has a hint of spice that will lift the flavour of the salmon and a touch of orange on the palate which matches perfectly with the orange jus.
This dish was Graham's award winning main course in the Spirit of Speyside Chef of the Year 2007 Competition.

Dauphinoise Potatoes
Preheat oven to 190C/Gas 5

This can be cooked the day before if necessary, and be warmed through before serving.

■ Take a shallow 20cm baking dish, butter the sides and rub with the garlic. Now neatly arrange the sliced potatoes and onions in alternate layers, seasoning each layer and ending with a layer of potatoes. Next add the vegetable stock and cover with tin foil. Place the dish in the oven for 35 – 40 minutes until the potatoes can be easily pierced with a sharp skewer.

■ Remove the foil and add 50ml double cream and place back in the oven to brown for a further 10 minutes, then remove from the oven and set aside.

Salmon
Preheat oven to 190C/Gas 5

■ Wash and then dry the salmon with a kitchen towel. Now dust the skin side with a little seasoned flour and pat off any excess. Set aside while you heat a large non stick pan with a little oil and butter. When hot, place the salmon skin side down in the pan, turn the heat down to medium and fry gently until the skin has browned. Sear the salmon on the remaining sides then transfer them to an ovenproof dish and place in oven for 5 - 8 minutes. The time will vary according to how you like your salmon cooked.

Sauce

■ In a heavy based sauté pan reduce the fish stock by ½ then add the Whisky and reduce by ½, now add the vegetable stock and reduce by ½. Add the orange juice and orange zest and reduce by a little. Add the honey to taste; it balances the bitterness of the whisky and the reduced orange.

■ Season with a little salt and pepper to taste.

You can prepare the sauce to this point earlier in the day and reheat ready to finish as below.

■ Just before serving whisk in a little unsalted butter to emulsify the sauce.

To Serve

■ Cut a slice of Dauphinoise potato and place on the centre of each plate, top with spring greens and then the salmon, skin side up. Pour a little sauce around the plate, decorating it with the black pudding and asparagus spears. Top the salmon with a little salmon roe or caviar then serve and wait for the applause!

Serves 4

Dauphinoise Potatoes
1 knob butter for greasing the baking dish
1 clove of garlic peeled
750g waxy potatoes peeled and finely sliced
1 medium onion, finely sliced
salt and freshly ground black pepper
100ml vegetable stock
50ml double cream

Salmon
4 fillets fresh salmon (approximately 175g each, skin on, scales removed. Ask your fishmonger to do this for you)
a little plain flour for dusting the salmon
salt and pepper for seasoning the flour
olive oil and butter for frying
50g salmon roe or caviar

Sauce
100ml Aberlour 16 year old Malt Whisky
100ml fish stock (or use a vegetable stock)
100ml vegetable stock
juice of 1 orange
pinch of orange zest
honey to taste
salt and pepper to season
a knob of unsalted butter

Vegetables and Garnish
12 baby asparagus spears, steamed lightly
175g spring greens washed and sliced - hard stalks removed, steamed and a little butter added plus salt and pepper and a pinch of grated nutmeg
2 slices of black pudding, cut into small triangles or cubes, fried until crisped.

Warm Smoked Mackerel Salad

The intensely spicy Tomintoul 10 year old is a perfect base for dressing any salad that utilises oily fish.

This healthy, low fat salad is unpretentious, no fussing with the presentation here, just mix it all together and enjoy! It is full of strong wonderful flavours which penetrate the potatoes because they are warm when you add the dressing. The dressing is creamy with a kick and so simple to make. A fantastic lunch or supper dish!

Serves 4

■ First boil the new potatoes in salted water until tender but not soft. Drain well and when dry but still warm cut into halves or chunks, place in a large warm bowl and set aside. While the potatoes are cooking, drop the green beans into boiling salted water and cook for 3-4 minutes until they tender but still fairly firm. Chop into 2cm pieces and add to the bowl with the potatoes. Warm the mackerel and the beetroot, break up the mackerel fillets and add to the potatoes and beans along with the beetroot. Now add the halved tomatoes and apples. Toss the mixture lightly together. Everything should feel warm but not hot.

■ Quickly mix all the dressing ingredients together in a jar with a lid and shake. Now pour the dressing on to your salad and toss it all together. It will be so colourful and will look so interesting. All you need to do now is scatter rocket leaves over the top and serve immediately.

■ Set the bowl in the middle of the table and allow your guests to help themselves.

The vegetables for this salad can be prepared in advance and warmed up just before putting them all together, adding the dressing and serving. If you decide to do this, cook the beans as above, then drain them and place in iced water, this will stop the cooking and retain the lovely bright green colour.

1kg new potatoes

50g green beans

4 peppered smoked mackerel fillets (or plain if you prefer)

16 cherry tomatoes (or baby plum tomatoes if you can get them), halved

3 eating apples, sliced or cut into bite sized pieces.

250g cooked beetroot, cut into fairly thick slices or chunks

Dressing
15mls Tomintoul 10 year old Malt Whisky

4 tablespoons horseradish sauce

60mls lemon juice

180mls olive oil, a good flavoured pure olive oil will be fine here

4 tablespoons Greek yoghurt

a pinch of caster sugar

salt and freshly ground black pepper

Garnish
fa few rocket leaves

Seared Halibut with Pea Sabayon and Pancetta

The full bodied, well-rounded Glen Moray 16 year old provides a very pleasing background note to this rich sauce and its sweetness is a vital link between the pea sabayon and the rest of the dish.

These flavours work so well together and create a very elegant dinner party dish. It is much easier to achieve than you might initially think because most of the elements can be prepared in advance.

Serves 4

Preheat the oven to 220C/Gas 6

◼ Heat a frying pan and gently fry the pancetta with the chopped shallot, then add the red wine and reduce by a third, add the beef stock and whisky and reduce by a further third. Season, pass through a sieve, return to a clean pan and set aside, reserving a few pieces of pancetta for decoration.

◼ Cook the potatoes, drain, return to the hot pan, dry and mash with butter until smooth. Meanwhile make the pea purée. Cook peas in boiling salted water, drain, mix in the butter and pass through a sieve or a mouli.*

◼ To cook the fish. Crush the fennel seeds and peppercorns in a pestle and mortar or in a bowl with the end of a rolling pin. Score the skin of the fish lightly with a sharp knife and rub both sides of the fish with a little olive oil. Sprinkle the crushed seeds, peppercorns and a little sea salt over the skin. Place the fish on a lightly oiled oven proof tray and cook in the oven, skin side up for 8 minutes.

◼ Whilst the fish is cooking, make the pea sabayon. Place the egg yolks and wine in a heatproof bowl and whisk over simmering water in a pan, do not allow the bowl to touch the water or it will split. Whisk until the mixture reaches ribbon stage (leaves a ribbon like trail from the whisk) then fold in the pea purée and season. Next wash the spinach, do not dry, place in a hot pan with butter, salt and pepper and a little grated nutmeg, cook gently until it is only just wilted.

*You can prepare to this point a few hours in advance and reheat.

To Serve

◼ Reheat the red wine sauce, add a knob of butter and whisk in. Place the pea sabayon in the centre of each plate, carefully place a mound of mashed potato in the middle of the sabayon, top with a spoonful of wilted spinach. Lay the fish skin side up on top of the spinach and finally trickle a little red wine sauce around the outside of the dish, place a few peas and the reserved pancetta decoratively in the sauce and serve. *Beautiful!*

Red Wine Sauce
a little olive oil for frying
50g diced pancetta
1 shallot, finely chopped
125mls red wine
125mls good beef stock
30mls Glen Moray 16 year old Malt Whisky
salt and freshly ground black pepper
a knob of butter for glazing

Fish
4 halibut fillets, 150g each, skin on
(you could use cod, turbot or other firm fleshed white fish)
1 teaspoon fennel seeds
1 teaspoon mixed dried peppercorns
1 tablespoon olive oil
sea salt
400g potatoes for mash

Pea Sabayon
200g peas plus a knob of butter
2 egg yolks
125mls dry white wine
salt and freshly ground black pepper

Wilted Spinach
100g baby spinach leaves
1 teaspoon butter
freshly grated nutmeg
salt and freshly ground black pepper

Garnish
a few cooked peas for each plate

Baked Nutty Salmon Parcels with Glengoyne and Tarragon

The clean taste of Glengoyne 10 year old, backed up by a hint of almonds and a sweet and malty finish balances perfectly with the bacon, almond and tarragon flavours coming through the salmon.

Cooking the salmon in a parcel is a wonderful method because it means that all the juices and flavours are retained. Some people like to serve this dish in the tinfoil but I prefer to remove it and its topping and place on a plate in the conventional manner. Am I just being boring?

Serves 4

Preheat oven to 200C/Gas mark 6

Melt the butter in a pan with a little olive oil and cook the onion gently until soft, add the bacon and cook for 2 minutes then stir in the tarragon, lemon juice and whisky. Now lay a large sheet of tinfoil in an ovenproof dish and place the salmon fillets on it, cover them with the onion mixture and sprinkle it with flaked almonds. Fold up the sides of the foil and seal to make a parcel. Place the dish in the oven and bake for 15 minutes.

To Serve

Carefully place a salmon fillet complete with topping in the centre of each plate topped with a small dollop of crème fraîche. Serve with new potatoes, blanched spinach and lightly cooked carrots on the side.

butter and olive oil for frying onion and bacon

1 small onion, finely chopped

2 rashers bacon, finely chopped

1 pinch dried tarragon or 1 sprig of fresh tarragon, chopped

50mls lemon juice

25mls Glengoyne 10 year old Malt Whisky

4 salmon fillets, seasoned with salt and pepper

25g blanched flaked almonds

Garnish
crème fraîche

You will need a large sheet of greased tinfoil and an oven proof dish.

Brown Trout in Oatmeal with Drambuie® Butter

Brown Trout or as they are known to fishermen "brownies" are caught in rivers and are tastier than the farmed Rainbow variety (unless they are organic). They are at their best from March to September. Herring in Oatmeal is a classic Scottish dish which goes back many generations and is very delicious, but treating river trout fillets in the same manner is equally wonderful. Serve it with Drambuie butter and you have something very special indeed.

Serves 4

■ Cut each skinned fillet of trout into four equal size pieces. Sprinkle with salt and pepper and dip each portion in milk and then coat with the oatmeal, pressing the oatmeal into the fish to ensure it is fully covered. Place the trout on a tray, cover with cling film and place in the fridge for twenty minutes.

■ To make the Drambuie Butter, warm the butter slightly to soften it but don't melt it and then beat in the other ingredients. Roll it into a log shape with a diameter of about 2½ cm / 1 inch and wrap it in cling film and leave it in the fridge or freezer for a while until it has firmed up.

■ Heat the olive oil in a non-stick frying pan, place the trout in the pan and cook for two minutes on each side or until the oatmeal is golden brown. Place 2 pieces of fish on each plate, cut 8 slices from the butter roll and place two on each fish immediately before serving. Any unused butter can be stored in the freezer.

2 large trout, skinned and filleted (brown or rainbow trout, whichever you can find)
salt and freshly ground black pepper
a little milk
100g medium oatmeal
90mls olive oil

Drambuie® Butter
125g unsalted butter
2 teaspoons lemon juice
1 tablespoon finely chopped flat leaf parsley
45mls Drambuie liqueur

Garnish
2 lemons cut into wedges
a bunch of watercress

To Serve
■ Arrange the trout on each serving plate with wedges of lemon, a little watercress, new potatoes and your favourite fresh vegetables.

Variation
■ Serve with a simple Dijon mustard sauce. (page 143)

Main Courses

Whisky Poached Salmon with a Whisky Butter Sauce

Aberlour 16 year old works so well with salmon we decided to use it more than once, its warm citrus notes will work with any fish dish.

This is a delicious dish which would be perfect for a spring or summer dinner party served with the new season's potatoes. The richness of the salmon is perfectly balanced by both the Aberlour and the lemony butter sauce.

Serves 4

4 salmon fillets, skin removed

■ To start, place all the poaching liquid ingredients into a pan, bring to a simmer and add the salmon steaks, cover the pan and poach very gently for 7-10 minutes, depending on the size of the steaks. Strain carefully, reserve the poaching liquid and place the salmon on a warm plate and keep them warm while you make the sauce.

■ Whisk the egg yolks and lemon juice in a small glass bowl then set it over a pan of hot water (not boiling) on a low heat. The bowl must not touch the water or the sauce will curdle. Whisk until the mixture begins to thicken then stir in the butter gradually. If mixture separates or any dry lumps appear, remove from the heat and add a teaspoon of cold water, then continue. When all of the butter is incorporated and the sauce is thickened, remove from heat and add the whisky and enough poaching liquid to retain a coating consistency. Return to the heat for a few minutes, whisking all the time. Add a little salt to taste.

To Serve

■ Coat the salmon with the sauce, garnish each with a sprig of dill or chives and serve with boiled new potatoes and fresh vegetables, lightly cooked courgettes or asparagus would be lovely.

Poaching liquid
120mls Aberlour16 year old Malt Whisky
120mls water
10 black peppercorns
2-3 bay leaves
1 small carrot, chopped
1 medium onion, finely chopped
1 stick celery, finely chopped
50mls lemon juice
2 sprigs of fresh thyme or 1 pinch dried thyme
salt and freshly ground black pepper

Sauce
2 egg yolks
25mls lemon juice
100g butter
15mls Aberlour16 year old Malt Whisky
30mls poaching liquid
salt to taste

Garnish
4 sprigs of fresh dill or chives

Main Courses

Hot Smoked Salmon Soufflé Tartlets

Delightfully seasoned by the Talisker 18 year old this dish will wow your dinner party friends.

It is a wonderful combination of my mum Ada's light fluffy soufflé and shortcrust pastry and when served with an avocado, caper and lemon salad and a little Talisker and Anchovy Cream, it makes a very unusual main course or starter. This would have really delighted her.

Hot smoked salmon differs from the more widely available cold smoked salmon, in that it is cooked during the smoking process. This results in a juicy, flaky fish that whilst having a smoky flavour, retains the characteristics of normally cooked fish. If you haven't tried it before, we highly recommend it. It is wonderful in salads, sandwiches, quiches, soufflées and with spaghetti, there are lots of possibilities.

Preheat the oven to 200C/Gas 6

■ To make the pastry, blend together the flour, butter, lard and water in a food processor to form a dough.

■ On a floured surface, roll out the pastry and line six greased tartlet cases. Line with greaseproof paper and baking beans and bake for 7 minutes. Remove the paper and baking beans and return the tartlets to the oven for a further 5 minutes until they crisp. Remove from the oven and leave to cool on a cooling rack.

Turn the oven heat down to 180C/Gas 5

■ To make the sauce, melt the butter in a sauce pan, stir in the flour and cook for about 1 minute then slowly stir in the milk and cook for about 2 minutes stirring all the time. Remove the sauce from the heat and add the cheese, horseradish sauce, whisky, lemon juice and two egg yolks and whisk to combine. Now add the smoked salmon and carefully stir into the sauce. Whisk the egg whites to stiff peaks then fold them carefully into the cheese mixture trying not to lose the air, check the seasoning and spoon into the pastry cases. Bake in the oven for 15 minutes until well risen and set.

■ For the salad, toss the salad leaves in the dressing and separately drizzle the dressing over the apples, avocado, beets and capers, ready to arrange on the plates.

To Serve

■ Place a tartlet on each plate and arrange the salad with the diced beetroot and capers scattered around it. Dress the plate with a little anchovy cream sauce and serve with a few new potatoes. *Totally Scrumptious!*

Serves 6

For The Pastry
200g plain flour, sifted
$^1/_2$ teaspoon salt
50g cold butter, cut into pieces
50g lard, cut into pieces
2 tablespoons ice cold water

Filling
25g butter
25g plain flour, sifted
300mls full cream milk
1 dessertspoonful horseradish cream
30mls Talisker 18 year old Malt Whisky
50g cream cheese, Crowdie is lovely but Philadelphia is fine
15mls lemon juice
4 eggs, separated. You will need 2 egg yolks and 4 egg whites
200g hot smoked salmon, skinned and flaked into bite sized pieces
salt and freshly ground black pepper, to season

Salad Dressing
juice of $^1/_2$ lemon, 4 tablespoons olive oil, $^1/_2$ teaspoon Dijon mustard, salt and pepper and a pinch of sugar whisked together

Salad
baby salad leaves
1 apple, peeled cored and sliced
2 ripe avocados sliced
2 teaspoons baby capers
2 baby beetroot, cooked and cut into small dice

Talisker™ and Anchovy Cream
(see page 48)
You could use horseradish sauce instead of the anchovy paste if you prefer, or a combination of both

You will need 6 individual 10cm tartlet cases and baking beans for baking blind.

Seared Hake with Shellfish and Garlic

Hazelburn 8 year old although young, has surprising depth and finish, its peppery notes and lingering, slightly malty finish deliver a pleasing background to the tasty sauce accompanying this delicious fish dish.

This is a fabulous dinner party dish with a terrific combination of flavours. We have used Hake but you can choose any fish with firm flesh, see what your fishmonger has to offer and make sure they leave the skin on. It is served quite simply with a wedge of crusty potato galette and some lovely peppery watercress.

Preheat oven to 220C/Gas 7

■ In a small bowl stir together the melted butter and the oil and use a little to brush the bottom and sides of an oven proof frying pan. Cut the potatoes thinly with a slicer and toss them in the butter and oil mixture. Working quickly to prevent the potatoes from discolouring, cover the base of the frying pan with a layer of the potato slices overlapping them quite tightly. Continue to layer the potatoes, seasoning them with salt and pepper.

■ Cook over a moderately high heat until it sizzles and the edges begin to brown. Now transfer the pan to the middle shelf of the oven and bake for 30 minutes or until the galette is golden and the potatoes are cooked. Remember that the pan handle will be extremely hot! When it is removed from the oven I always keep a cloth on the handle until I am finished with the pan to remind me.

If you don't have a frying pan that is suitable for the oven, use a non stick frying pan, follow the instructions above and then you can continue on the top of the stove, but you will need to cover the pan with a lid and turn the heat down to low. Cook for 10 minutes and then to cook the other side, slide the galette on to a large plate. Place the frying pan upside down on top of the galette and holding the plate and pan tightly, flip the galette back into the pan. Now cook for a further 10 minutes or so until the potatoes are tender.

■ Whilst the potatoes are cooking, scrub the cockles and mussels (treat the cockles the same as the mussels, see page 121) and put them into a pan with the white wine, whisky and water. Cover and cook for about 3 minutes, shaking the pan occasionally until they open. Drain over a bowl to collect the juices. When they have cooled a little remove the meat from most of the shells. Set aside. Return the cooking liquid to the pan and add 200mls water and boil to reduce to about 2 tablespoons and set aside.

■ Now to make the sauce, crush the garlic cloves and add to the food processor with the rest of the sauce ingredients and whizz until combined. Set aside.

Serves 4

Potato Galette
100g unsalted butter, melted
2 tablespoons vegetable oil
750g potatoes, preferably baking, peeled
salt and freshly ground black pepper

Shellfish
500g cockles
500g mussels
50mls dry white wine
1 teaspoon Hazelburn 8 year old Malt Whisky
200mls water

Garlic Butter Sauce
2 plump cloves of garlic
100g unsalted butter
1 teaspoon lemon juice
1 teaspoon Hazelburn 8 year old Malt Whisky
1 tablespoon fresh flat leaf parsley, finely chopped
salt and freshly ground black pepper
4 x 175g pieces of thick hake fillets, skin on (halibut, cod or turbot will also work well)
25g butter and a little olive oil for frying
150g small prawns or shrimps, cooked and peeled

Garnish
a bunch of watercress

You will need an 20cm/8 or 9 inch frying pan with a metal handle suitable for the oven.*

Seared Hake with Shellfish and Garlic (continued)

■ When you are nearly ready to serve, season the hake on both sides. Heat a large non stick frying pan with the butter and oil and fry the fish skin side down for about 3 minutes on a moderate heat, turn the fish over and cook the other side for about 2 minutes. Remove from the pan and put on an oven proof tray and place in the oven for a further 3 minutes, switch off the heat and allow it to cook in the residual heat of the pan.

■ Meanwhile, melt the garlic butter mixture in a pan with the reduced cooking liquid from the shellfish, add the prawns and the shellfish and stir in. Cook gently until it is all warmed through.

To Serve

■ Place the hake, skin side up on to warmed serving plates and spoon the shellfish sauce over and around the fish. Serve this with the potato galette cut into wedges, and a few sprigs of watercress. *Perfect!*

Bunnahabhain™ Mussels with Strathdon Blue Cheese

The peatiness of Bunnahabhain 12 year old, although not as evident as in other Islay malts, contrasts really well with the strong, creamy Strathdon Blue.

Mussels are a wonderful food with a delicate taste, they are high in protein and low in cholesterol and fat. In fact mussels contain higher levels of Omega-3 fatty acids than any other shellfish so they are very good for keeping your heart and brain healthy. They are at their best in cold weather hence the old saying only to eat them when there is an "r" in the month i.e. September to April. Also British mussels spawn in April so they are very small in the summer months.

When you buy mussels, make sure that they only smell of the sea and don't have a fishy smell. Their shells should be shiny blue/black in colour and do not buy mussels which are broken or gaping open. When you clean them, if they are open and do not close when you tap the shell sharply with your knife, they are dead so you must discard them. The meat will range from bright orange to a pale cream colour, but this is not an indication of quality - orange flesh simply tells you it's a female while the paler mussel is a male or an immature female.

There are lots of lovely sauces to serve mussels in but this one is a particularly wonderful combination. I hope you will enjoy it!

Serves 4

■ Clean the mussels by scrubbing them, removing their beards and rinsing several times to remove any sand or grit. Discard any broken mussels or those that do not close when tapped sharply. Set aside.

■ Melt the butter in a large pan with the olive oil and cook the shallots and garlic over a medium heat until transparent. Stir frequently to prevent browning then add the remaining ingredients except the mussels and reduce by half. Taste, adding a little more whisky if desired.

■ Add the mussels, turn the heat up high and put the lid on. Cook for about 2-3 minutes shaking the pan periodically, until all the mussels have opened. Discard any that do not open.

■ Finally sprinkle in the chopped parsley and add the knob of butter.

To Serve

■ Serve in warmed bowls with crusty bread on the side to mop up the delicious soup.

■ Provide a finger bowl and a spare bowl for the discarded shells.

2kg fresh mussels
50g butter and a little olive oil
6 shallots, chopped
2-4 cloves of garlic, chopped
300mls white wine
1 large sprig thyme
50mls Bunnahabhain 12 year old Malt Whisky
200ml double cream
50g Strathdon blue cheese (Roquefort or other creamy blue cheese could be used instead)
salt and lots freshly ground black pepper
couple of shakes of lemon juice
50g fresh flat leaf parsley, chopped

Garnish
50g fresh flat leaf parsley, finely chopped
1 knob of butter

You will need a deep pan a with tight fitting lid.

Main Courses

Mussels with Linguine and Talisker Single Malt Scotch Whisky™

Talisker 18 year old's strong peppery flavour and robust finish provides delicious seasoning for this dish.
Another wonderful recipe using these delicious little shellfish, this time we have paired them with Talisker but cooked them Italian style. The Talisker works so well with the lightly spiced tomato sauce.

■ Start by scrubbing the mussels clean, removing the beards and rinsing in clean water several times to remove any sand or grit. Discard any broken mussels or those that do not close when tapped sharply. Set aside.
■ Now melt the butter in a large pan with the oil and gently sauté the shallots and garlic until transparent then add the white wine and reduce by a half. Add the mussels and parsley, turn the heat up high, put the lid on the pan and cook for 2-3 minutes, shaking the pan occasionally until all the mussels open, discard any that do not open. Strain the mussels and reserve the cooking liquid. Set the mussels aside.
■ Meanwhile make the sauce. Heat the olive oil in a pan and add the shallots, garlic and chilli pepper, cook gently for about 4 minutes until the shallots are transparent. Now add the tomatoes, balsamic vinegar, sugar, whisky and half of the reserved cooking liquid. Bring to the boil and cook for 8-10 minutes until the sauce reduces and thickens. Taste and season with salt, freshly ground black pepper and basil.
■ While the sauce is cooking, cook the linguine according to the instructions on the pack. When only just cooked (al dente), drain and stir into the sauce. Now remove half of the mussels from their shells and add the mussel meat to the sauce, along with the remaining mussels in their shells.

To Serve
■ Place the linguine and mussel sauce in warmed bowls sprinkled with a little grated parmesan and chopped parsley and with crusty bread on the side.
■ Provide a finger bowl and a spare bowl for the discarded shells. You will probably also need large napkins!

Serves 4

2kg fresh mussels
50g butter and a little olive oil
6 shallots or a medium onion, chopped
2 cloves garlic, finely chopped
300mls dry white wine
1 tablespoon finely chopped fresh flat leaf parsley

Sauce
1 tablespoon olive oil
6-8 shallots, peeled and divided into their cloves or cut into chunks
2 cloves garlic, finely chopped
$^1/_2$ red chilli pepper, deseeded and finely chopped
1 x 400g tin chopped tomatoes
30mls balsamic vinegar
25g demerara sugar
50mls Talisker 18 year old Malt Whisky
salt and freshly ground black pepper
fresh basil leaves

Pasta
225g linguine or any ribbon pasta, dried or fresh

Garnish
25g grated parmesan cheese
1 tablespoon finely chopped fresh flat leaf parsley
Crusty Bread

Main Courses

Savoury Bread and Butter Pudding

The complex toasted malt background of Glenmorangie 10 year old works really well with Starthdon Blue Cheese. This is an example of neighbours getting along as they are both made in the same highland town of Tain.

Surprise your non meat eating friends with this unusual and very tasty dish. It is surprisingly light and can be served as a starter or a main course. Here it is cooked in individual ramekins for a main course but you could bake it in 8 smaller dishes and then serve them as starters. The autumnal, earthy flavour of the chanterelles works so well with the Strathdon cheese and the Glenmorangie complements them both.

Serves 4-6

Preheat oven 200C/Gas 6

- Heat a frying pan, add the olive oil and butter and gently fry the chopped shallot until soft, add the garlic and cook for a further minute. Add the chanterelles to the pan and cook for about 2 minutes. Meanwhile lightly grease 4 ramekins with butter and set aside. Begin by placing a disc of butter soaked bread in the base of each ramekin. Now half fill the ramekins with some mushrooms and cheese and another layer of butter soaked bread, repeat so that each has two layers, finishing with final disc of butter soaked bread.
- Now make the egg custard. Whisk the eggs in a large bowl until fluffy. Place the milk, cream, thyme and whisky in a saucepan and heat to just below boiling point. Remove from the heat, pour over the eggs and whisk well. Season well with salt and pepper. Strain the mixture into a jug, and then carefully pour over the bread, pressing the bread gently down into the custard. Add more custard until the bread is saturated. Leave to soak for at least 30 minutes, if you have any mixture left over add it a little at a time until it won't take any more.*
- Bake in the oven for 20-25 minutes until risen and golden brown. The bread that is out of the custard will become crisp and will contrast nicely with the soft pudding underneath.

a little olive oil and small piece of butter for frying
1 shallot, finely chopped
1 clove of garlic, crushed
100g chanterelle mushrooms
1 small thin sliced white loaf or a baguette
100g butter, melted
100g Strathdon blue cheese, crumbled
5 eggs
120mls milk
120mls double cream
1 pinch dried thyme
30mls Glenmorangie 10 year old Malt Whisky
salt and freshly ground black pepper to taste

To Serve
- Arrange on the serving plate with a fresh vegetable salad of mixed leaves, apple, celery, walnuts and cooked, chilled asparagus and broad beans dressed with vinaigrette.
- If serving as a starter prepare a salad of mixed leaves, celery, apple, pomegranate seeds and walnuts dressed in vinaigrette. It works beautifully with the flavours of the pudding.

*Make to this stage up to 24 hours in advance and store in the fridge until you are ready to bake and serve.

Variations
- This Savoury Pudding is also very delicious made with the summer flavours of sun blush tomatoes, 2 in each pudding; pepperdews, 1 in each pudding; mozzarella, 2 thick slices in each pudding; and basil, at least 2 leaves in each pudding instead of the blue cheese, mushrooms and thyme. Then serve with a salsa made with red pepper, red onion, chilli, tomato, caper, and basil.

Main Courses

Linguine with Strathdon and Walnut Sauce

The big nutty and spicy undertones, combined with obvious sherry notes make The Macallan 10 year old another perfect match for the strong creamy Strathdon Blue Cheese.
This is our Scottish take on a well known Italian dish. It can either be served as a starter or a main course and I'm sure that you will agree that this is a delicious combination of flavours.

Serves 4

450g linguine
15mls olive oil
100g walnuts, roughly chopped
salt and freshly ground black pepper
300mls double cream
25mls The Macallan 10 year old Malt Whisky
100g Strathdon blue cheese
2 plump garlic cloves, crushed
2 teaspoons lemon juice

■ Cook the linguine in a large saucepan of boiling salted water until only just tender *(al dente)*. Drain immediately and return to the pan with a little olive oil, walnuts, salt and pepper, mix together and keep warm.
■ While the linguine is cooking make the sauce. Put the cream into a pan add the whisky, the Strathdon cheese, crushed garlic and lemon juice and heat gently, stirring well until the cheese is almost all melted. Season with salt and pepper.

To Serve
■ Pour the sauce into the linguine and toss until it is all combined. Serve immediately in warmed bowls with a dressed mixed salad of green leaves and apple.

Just wonderful!

Variations
■ Tagliatelle or Spaghetti Verdi, or any ribbon pasta are excellent alternative pastas to choose. You could also vary the cheese, we have suggested the Scottish Strathdon Blue, but Roquefort or Gorganzola could also be used.

Paw Paw Pitta Pockets

The unmistakeable rummy notes which come through at all levels of the BenRiach 15 year old Dark Rum Wood are the perfect match for this dish with its Caribbean roots.
Believe me you don't have to be veggie to appreciate the incredible flavours in this dish. It is very unusual and was inspired by a meaty Jamaican baked paw paw recipe that my brother Gordon gave me.

Serves 6-8

■ Cook the lentils in boiling salted water for about 30 minutes until tender but still firm, drain and set aside. Meanwhile cut the paw paws in half lengthwise, scoop out and discard the seeds. Scoop out all the flesh, chop and set aside. Now heat a frying pan with the olive oil and cook the onion and garlic gently until transparent. Add the lentils and all of the other ingredients except the whisky. Stir occasionally until the carrots are cooked but still crisp, the mixture is thick and most of the liquid has evaporated. Add the whisky, and cook for a few minutes, taste and season well.

200g green lentils
3-4 paw paws, depending on size (papaya)
1 tablespoon olive oil
1 medium onion, finely chopped
1 plump garlic clove, crushed
1 large carrot, diced
175g black eye beans (300g tin, drained)
400g tin chopped tomatoes
1/2 teaspoon ground allspice
1 tablespoon tomato purée
30mls BenRiach Dark Rum Wood Finish 15 year old Malt Whisky
salt and freshly ground black pepper

To Serve
■ Stuff the pitta bread pockets with salad and then fill with the paw paw mixture and top with crème fraîche. If you want to make this dish vegan, you just need to ensure that the pitta is vegan and omit the crème fraîche. *Still fantastic!*

Variations
■ You can serve this with deep fried banana fritters, flavoured with allspice. Yum...You could also replace the pitta bread with tortilla wraps.
■ If you do not allow the mixture to become quite so thick, if necessary adding some vegetable stock, you have a sauce which is wonderful over pasta, topped with crème fraîche and served with a side salad. It also makes an awesome lasagne, topped with vegetarian parmesan style cheese. *Enjoy!*

To Serve
12 pitta breads
salad leaves
cucumber
red pepper, sliced
crème fraîche

Main Courses

Gratin of Saffron Braised Fennel

Hazelburn 8 year old's complexity and unmissable peppery notes are wonderful in this flavoursome combination. This is a delicious dish which can be served as a main course as here or it is fantastic as an accompaniment to fish or white meat dishes. Fennel is a Mediterranean vegetable which we are less familiar with in the UK, but I love it. The long slow cooking in this recipe brings out the natural sweetness and slightly aniseed flavour of the fennel. If you've never eaten it before or haven't been sure about it, try this dish, it has converted many people who thought they didn't like fennel. I first had braised fennel in France hiding under a wonderful piece of cod and I came home and tried to recreate it. Hope you love it too!

Serves 6

6 fennel bulbs
2 medium onions
3 medium carrots
3 sticks of celery
olive oil
2 plump cloves of garlic, crushed
1 sprig of thyme
2 bay leaves
grated rind of ¹/₂ small orange
300mls dry white wine
1 large pinch saffron
30-50mls Hazelburn 8 year old Malt Whisky (to taste)
salt and freshly ground black pepper

Preheat oven to 180C/Gas 4

▪ Cut the long stems from the top of the fennel, cut the bulbs in half and then cut away the tough core. Blanch in boiling salted water for 2 minutes and leave to cool.

▪ Meanwhile finely dice the onions, carrots and celery. Heat a casserole dish or roasting pan with a little olive oil and gently sweat the onions, carrots, celery and crushed garlic. When they have sweated well, lay the fennel on top. Add the thyme, bay leaves and grated orange rind. Mix the saffron with the white wine and whisky and pour into the pan. Add sufficient water to cover the vegetables. Bring to the boil, season with salt and pepper. Cover and cook in the oven for 2 hours.

▪ Meanwhile, parboil the potatoes in boiling salted water until almost cooked. Drain and cool so that you can handle them. When cool enough to handle, slice them thinly and set aside.

Topping

4 baking potatoes
25mls melted butter
90g gruyere cheese, grated

You will need a roasting pan and a tin foil cover or a casserole dish suitable for the hob.

Turn oven up to 200C/Gas 6

▪ When the fennel is cooked, lay the potato slices overlapping on top of the fennel, season, drizzle with melted butter and sprinkle with the grated cheese. Place in the oven and bake for about 20-30 minutes until the potatoes are tender and the cheese is browned.

To Serve

▪ If you have cooked this in an oven-to-table dish you can serve it from the dish on the table. Serve with some fresh green vegetables or a crisp green salad.

Variation

▪ You can omit the potatoes and then serve as a side dish with fish or chicken.

Main Courses

Medley of Roasted Winter Vegetables

Hazelburn 8 year old stands out as a perfect match for this dish creating a delightfully flavoursome layer of taste. This is a very colourful, tasty dish which is very versatile because it can be served as a veggie main course when accompanied by Yorkshire puddings, mustard or horseradish sauce and vegetarian gravy or as an accompaniment to many meat dishes. This recipe is dedicated to my daughters Rachel and Jennifer who love their vegetables. It is warming and filling and tastes as good as it looks!

Preheat oven to 200C/Gas 6

▨ To roast the vegetables, heat the oil in a large roasting tin until very hot. With the roasting pan on the heat on the hob, add the onions, shallots, carrots, neeps, and white potatoes and turn in the oil, then cook for a few minutes without turning so that they begin to brown. Add the remaining ingredients, turn them all gently then cover the tin with foil and bake for 20 minutes.

▨ Meanwhile mix all the sauce ingredients together and place in a small serving bowl.

▨ Remove the foil and turn over all the vegetables. Add the cooked beetroot, and return to the top of the oven for 10-15 minutes until the vegetables are tender and golden brown.

▨ To make a delicious gravy to enjoy with the vegetables see page 134.

▨ Mix all of the Mustard or Horseradish Sauce ingredients together and it's ready to serve.

Preheat oven to 220C/Gas 7

▨ For the Vegan Yorkshire Puddings, place a teaspoon vegetable fat in each of the bun tins and heat in the oven for 10 minutes until very hot. Meanwhile, sieve the flour with the salt. Mix the milk, yoghurt and lemon juice together. Make a well in the centre of the flour and then gradually add the milk mixture, stirring in to combine. Beat well with a whisk, adding more milk as necessary until the batter is the consistency of cream. Remove the tin carefully from the oven and place on the heat on the hob, pour the batter into the tins and bake for 20-25 minutes until risen and brown. Try to resist opening the oven before 20 minutes. They tend not to rise as high as those made with eggs but they are delicious none-the-less.

Serves 6

4 tablespoons vegetable oil

2 red onions peeled root still intact, quartered

6 peeled shallots, left whole

4 medium carrots, scrubbed and cut into chunks

225g swede (neeps) cut into chunks

225g small potatoes scrubbed and halved

1 large parsnip peeled and cut into chunks

1 sweet potato peeled and cut into chunks

4 sticks celery, cut into fairly large pieces

4-6 garlic cloves peeled and left whole

1/2 red chilli, chopped

4 sprigs fresh rosemary or 2 pinches dried

salt and freshly ground black pepper

8 cooked fresh baby beetroot, cut in half (added towards the end of the cooking time)

Mustard or Horseradish Sauce
omit for vegan version

100mls sour cream or crème fraîche

1 teaspoon mustard of your choice or 1 tablespoon creamed horseradish

5mls Hazelburn 8 year old Malt Whisky (or more to taste)

1 tablespoon chopped fresh chives

salt and freshly ground black pepper

Veggie Gravy
see page 134

Vegan Yorkshire Puddings
solid white vegetable fat for the tins

125g self raising flour

1/2 tsp salt

150mls soya or rice milk

150mls natural soya yoghurt

1 teaspoon lemon juice

You will need a 6 cup size bun tray.

Lentil Mealie Pudding

The delicious oak character of Glenfarclas 15 year old with its lightly spiced, smoky finish works well with this clever vegetarian alternative to haggis.

This steamed pudding is a lovely combination of flavours and textures, it makes a tasty, healthy lunch or supper dish with a plain or whisky gravy accompanied by vegetables and you don't have to be vegetarian to enjoy it. It is also a big favourite with my veggie daughters as a Haggis substitute on Burns Night. It is very straightforward and no offal in sight! I have tried lots of recipes for vegetarian haggis and this is definitely the tastiest!

Serves 4

■ Place the lentils in a bowl, cover with cold water and set aside until you have finished preparing the vegetables. Chop the onions and carrots into fine dice. Now put about 8cm / 3inches of hot water in a large pan and bring to the boil on a medium heat.

■ Drain the lentils through a sieve and rinse with cold water, then put them in a mixing bowl. Add all the other ingredients and stir well with a wooden spoon, check the seasoning, you may need to add more pepper. Now scrape the mixture into a medium sized pudding basin and smooth the top with the back of a spoon. Cover the bowl with tin foil and fix tightly round the edges. Lower carefully into the pan of boiling water.

■ Reduce the heat so that the water is just bubbling and then put the lid on the pan. Steam for 3 hours, checking every hour to make sure the water is not boiling away. Add more water as necessary.

■ Meanwhile make the gravy, heat a frying pan and add the oil and fry the onion gently for about 5 minutes, then add the flour and cook for a further 5-10 minutes until the mixture turns light brown and the onion is well cooked. Add the crushed garlic, cook for 2 minutes then gradually add the stock and whisky. Bring to the boil and simmer for 10 minutes. Strain through a sieve into a clean saucepan, add the remaining ingredients and season to taste, stir well and it is ready to serve.

To Serve

■ Serve with gravy, potatoes and vegetables, or of course you can serve it with mashed potatoes and mashed neeps (swede) for an alternative Burns Night dish.

The Pudding

50g red lentils

2 medium onions

2 large carrots

225g medium oatmeal

50g chopped mixed nuts

1 plump clove of garlic, crushed

2 large pinches dried thyme

1 teaspoon yeast extract

120mls warm water

30mls Glenfarclas 15 year old Malt Whisky

2¹/₂ teaspoons salt

several turns of freshly ground black pepper

Vegetarian Whisky Gravy

1 medium onion, peeled and chopped

2 tablespoons olive oil

2 tablespoons plain flour

1 plump clove garlic, crushed

500mls vegetable stock, (preferably a dark vegetable stock page 145)

30mls Glenfarclas 15 year old Malt Whisky (optional)

¹/₂ teaspoon yeast extract

2 tablespoons soy sauce

salt and freshly ground black pepper

Green Lentil, Carrot and Walnut Salad

Auchentoshan Three Wood's spicy, nutty background brings out all the flavours in this crunchy, nutty salad.

This salad always reminds me of our holidays in the Languedoc in France. We have adapted it here with a whiskied walnut vinaigrette. It is a salad but it is quite filling and there's no lettuce... It is crunchy, fresh tasting, extremely healthy and I think best served cold.

Serves 4

■ Put the lentils into a large bowl with the carrots, walnuts, garlic, spring onions, tomato dice and vinaigrette. Mix well, season with salt and pepper and leave to marinate for several hours.

225g green lentils, cooked and drained
2 carrots, peeled and very finely diced
50g walnuts, fairly finely chopped
2 plump garlic cloves, crushed
8 spring onions, trimmed and finely chopped
2 tomatoes skinned and de seeded, then chopped into fine dice
4 hard boiled eggs
salt and freshly ground black pepper

To Serve

■ This recipe can be served as a starter or a main course. As a starter this recipe serves 6-8. Just sprinkle with fresh parsley and decorate with wedges of boiled egg. For a casual lunch for 4 people, spoon all the salad heaped up into a lovely bowl and refrigerate until you are ready to serve. Then sprinkle the parsley on top and surround the salad with the hard boiled eggs, shelled and cut into wedges and invite your guests to help themselves.

Variations

■ This recipe works well with puy lentils or other continental lentils. It will not work with red lentils because they do not stay whole when cooked.

■ You could lightly cook all the vegetables and serve it warm either as a main course dish or omit the eggs and serve as an accompaniment to meat or fish dishes. Lots of other diced vegetables can be added like celery, sweet peppers and courgettes and of course the nuts can be varied or omitted to your taste. Try this with some lettuce, cucumber and tomato in a wrap or pitta bread.

■ It is also lovely with fried diced pancetta mixed through the salad as a non veggie option.

Vinaigrette

Auchentoshan Three Wood Malt Whisky
20mls red wine vinegar
75mls walnut oil
2 teaspoons salt
freshly ground black pepper
pinch of sugar to taste

Garnish

2 tablespoonfuls of fresh chopped flat leaf parsley

Highland Region

The Highland whisky region extends from Dundee in the east and Greenock in the south west to Scotland's most northerly point at John O'Groats. The rugged landscapes, wild coastlines and variable climate contribute to the wide variations of flavour found in Highland whiskies. It is impossible to generalise about their characteristics. Some are dry and grassy, some have the unmistakable scent of heather, others are sweet and fruity, reminiscent of Speyside malts and some of the west coast Highland malts have a smoky background not unlike their Islay neighbours.

Travelling north along the A9, the mountains rise up from the horizon in a series of spectacular views that change with every turn of the road. In late autumn the drive from Perth to Pitlochry is nothing short of fantastic, the season brings changing colours to the trees which present the traveller with an infinitely varied palate of rich autumn colours, which must rate amongst the most beautiful vistas on the planet. Just 1 mile outside Pitlochry lies Scotland's smallest distillery. Edradour Malt Whisky is still produced here using the original 150 year old equipment but only produces 12 casks a week at full production, making it a rare find on the malt shelf of any bar or supermarket. The visitor centre always has stock though so if you are passing why not call in and you'll be welcomed with a "dram" in the Malt Barn.

Continuing north along the A9, turn west at Dalwhinnie, maybe stopping off at the distillery before heading for the A86 and Fort William. The road eventually descends from Spean Bridge and sitting at the end of Loch Linnhe is Fort William. Its impressive neighbour; the UK's highest mountain Ben Nevis, looks over the bustling loch side town which offers a huge range of services. Not to be missed is the Ben Nevis Distillery at the foot of the mountain. Heading west again you will find yourself on "the road to the isles".

The road passes through Glenfinnan, which provided the location for the filming of the railway viaduct scenes for the hit film, *Harry Potter, The Prisoner of Azkaban*. During filming, the sparks from the Hogwarts Express set the heather moorland alight between Fort William and Mallaig, and fire fighters battled for many hours to put out the fire.

When you arrive at the working port of Mallaig take a walk around the town and harbour, there are all too few small fishing ports left in Scotland, so make the most of your visit. Although a relatively new town as it did not really exist until the early 20th century, Mallaig is a fascinating place. If you are lucky enough to arrive at the harbour at the same time as the fishing fleet docks, you might get the chance to bargain with the crew for something for tonight's table. Failing that, take a look at Andy Race's Fish shop. Andy has an amazing array of top quality fresh and smoked fish, his kippers alone are worth a detour, and if you are visiting during the sprat season, January to March, get a packet of his smoked Sprats, take them home, brush with a little butter and grill lightly for a real treat.

Heading back towards Spean Bridge turn north on the A82 for Inverness. As the road drops into Fort Augustus the visitor is immediately faced with the impressive view of the town's Benedictine abbey, no monks these days but still an imposing sight. Bisected by the Caledonian Canal, Fort Augustus is a busy tourist town with plenty to offer the visitor. There's the canal heritage centre, the clansman centre and lots of shops and places to eat. Most importantly though, the town marks the entry to the Caledonian Canal proper and the southern shores of Loch Ness, the most famous body of inland water in the world.

Time to get out the camera again as you head north along the western shore of Loch Ness, a photo of Nessie would make you a very rich person, so keep a careful eye out. Loch Ness offers everything for all types of visitor - fantastic scenery, boat trips, Urquhart Castle, Loch Ness 2000 Exhibition, fishing and of course Nessie watching.

At the northernmost end of Loch Ness the road follows the parallel paths of the Caledonian Canal and the River Ness into Inverness, capital of the Scottish Highlands. This compact highland city, set on the Moray Firth, astride the River Ness and overlooked by the castle is one of our favourite Scottish cities. The capital abounds with great restaurants and a typical highland welcome awaits you in all of the city's many bars, museums, galleries, shopping outlets and tourist attractions. Check out Eden Court Theatre, newly refurbished, the theatre always has quality productions on offer whatever time of the year. There used to be two distilleries in the city but alas they are both closed.

Inverness is the gateway to the north and west Highlands of Scotland. The road continues north following the rugged coastline past Glenmorangie Distillery in Tain, definitely worth a visit, towards John O'Groats, finally ending at the last house on the Scottish mainland. The last time we took some friends to John O'Groats, all they talked

Salmon

about was having their photograph taken next to the famous signpost but sadly we got there the day after the signpost had been stolen! Nearby is the historic Castle of Mey, the northernmost residence of the late Queen Elizabeth the Queen Mother. The newly established visitor centre and in particular, the gardens are a real treat.

North west of Inverness the road climbs through Wester Ross out of Strathpeffer and over Beinn Dearg, "Red Hill" before descending into Ullapool and the shores of Loch Broom. The town is a picturesque fishing village which is also the departure port for the ferry to Stornoway. In addition to the usual facilities and entertainment found in highland towns, Ullapool has a fast growing reputation for excellent music festivals.

Lying east of Inverness is the Cathedral City of Elgin, birthplace of the inventor Alexander Graham Bell. Elgin is steeped in history, reflected in its restored 18th century town houses and wynds and the remains of the beautiful cathedral, sadly now in ruins. The cathedral was sacked in the 14th century by the ruthless and barbaric son of Robert II, Alexander Stewart, The Wolf of Badenoch. Popular with all visitors is Johnstons Visitor Centre. The name Johnstons is synonymous with the finest quality luxury cashmere in the world. The mill in Elgin is the only mill in Scotland to transform cashmere from fibre to finished article. You can take a free guided tour of the entire process with one of the centre's expert guides.

Glen Moray, although technically a Speyside malt, is worthy of a mention whilst we are discussing Elgin. The whisky is made in a small authentic working distillery without the tourist frills, just bags of atmosphere and real people going about their business – making whisky. Here you have the opportunity to experience the reality of malt whisky distilling. The delight of Glen Moray is that your tour guide could be one of the distillery craftsmen themselves, the stillman, mashman or even the manager.

Following the moray coast eastwards brings you into a relatively undiscovered corner of Scotland, where the sprawling coastline and vast empty beaches are punctuated with picturesque fishing villages and dramatic cliff tops, just waiting to be explored. The Grampians and Aberdeenshire abound with trails of discovery. Wonderful castles, distilleries and prehistoric stone circles litter the region all the way down to Aberdeen.

The Granite City, Aberdeen, boasts a magnificent skyline and the granite buildings, after which it is named, glisten and sparkle after the rain. Originally a busy fishing and trading port, this has now been overtaken by the booming oil industry - many of the world's leading companies have their UK headquarters in Aberdeen. The prosperity associated with the industry is evident throughout the city with an abundance of shops, top quality restaurants and friendly bars as well as theatres, music venues, galleries and museums. To top it all, the beach esplanade boasts a huge range of great facilities for the kids too.

The Highland region covers such a vast area of such beauty and interest that we can only touch upon it in this short piece so we would encourage you to come and discover it for yourselves.

Highland Region

Highland Green Peppercorn Cream - *Photographed opposite*

Highland Park 12 year old's heathery, spicy, smooth and honeyed tones create an underlying flavoursome layer to this sauce, which works equally well with steaks, pork or lamb's liver. This simple little sauce brings a delicious touch of spiciness to whatever meat you are cooking and will become a firm favourite. You can make this sauce whilst your steaks are cooking, or you can have it made in advance, it will even keep in the fridge for a few days.

Serves 4

■ Reduce the beef stock by half, add the red wine and further reduce by half, add the whisky and green peppercorns and simmer for a few minutes. Finally add the cream and season with salt and pepper. Simmer until the sauce has thickened sufficiently. Check the seasoning and serve.

500mls beef stock
250mls red wine
25mls Highland Park 12 year old Malt Whisky
1 tablespoon green peppercorns in brine (drained)
200mls double cream
salt and freshly ground black pepper

Red Onion Marmalade - *Photographed on pages 32 and 36*

The presence of sherry notes at all levels in Aberlour a'bunadh make an excellent base for this marmalade which is wonderful with cheeses, pâtés, steaks, cold meats and sausages. It is very versatile, try adding a spoonful to gravies and sauces for a lovely caramelised onion flavour.

■ Cut the onions in half lengthwise and then slice quite finely. Now fry them gently in the olive oil until softened, then add the remaining ingredients and bring to the boil. Reduce the heat slightly and continue to cook until the mixture has reduced and most of the liquid has evaporated. Allow to cool a little and bottle in sterilized jars.
■ You can also pack it into an airtight container and it will keep in the fridge for several weeks.

1.5 kg red onions
40mls olive oil
225g soft brown sugar
225mls balsamic vinegar
225mls red wine
30g sultanas (optional)
50mls Aberlour a'bunadh cask strength Malt Whisky

Accompaniments & Sauces

Whisky Madeira Sauce

Black Bottle Blended Scotch Whisky lends an interesting layer to this versatile sauce.

This is a very useful sauce to serve with meat but can also be paired with the meatier fish and even with vegetable dishes.

■ Heat frying pan with a little olive oil and gently cook the shallots and mushrooms until the shallots are transparent. Add the whisky and Madeira, increase the heat and reduce by a half. Strain and add the stock and reduce again by a further half, add the cream, thyme, parsley and seasoning and bring back to the boil. Add the meat juices if you have any then when you are ready to serve add the butter a little at a time and whisk it in.

Variation
■ Omit the cream and you have a wonderful reduced sauce, full of flavour.

Makes 300mls

olive oil for frying
2 shallots, finely chopped (about 100g)
4 mushrooms, finely chopped (about 50g)
30mls Black Bottle Blended Scotch Whisky
200mls Madeira wine
500mls good beef stock
75mls double cream
1 pinch dried thyme
1 dessertspoon fresh flat leaf parsley, chopped
salt and freshly ground black pepper
50g butter

Saffron Sauce - *Photographed with Mussel Tart*

Arran 10 year old's strong citrus notes and hint of spice sit very well with the wine, lemon and pepper flavours of this useful sauce.

This delightful sauce is like a splash of sunshine. It is lovely with so many dishes, mussel tart, vegetables such as asparagus and broad beans; chicken; veal; white fish; scallops; oysters, in fact all shellfish.

■ Place the saffron in a bowl and pour the hot water over it, set aside. Finely chop the onion or shallots and place them in a saucepan with the wine and whisky. Bring to the boil and simmer until it is reduced to one tablespoon. Remove from the heat, stir in the cream then place back on the heat and simmer until it has reduced by about a half. Remove from the heat again and whisk in the butter a little at a time. Stir in the saffron water and lemon juice and season with salt and pepper. Sieve out the onions, to create a beautiful smooth sauce. If you need to keep it warm, sieve it into a heatproof bowl and place over a pan of barely simmering water. If it gets too hot it will split, if this does occur, don't worry, just remove from the heat and whisk in some cold cream and you should be able to recover it.

1 pinch of saffron threads
20mls hot water
1 small onion or 2 shallots
150ml dry white wine
20mls Arran 10 year old Malt Whisky
150 ml double cream
100g unsalted butter
2 teaspoons lemon juice
salt and freshly ground black pepper

Rhubarb and Ginger Chutney

- Photographed with Lanark Blue and Caramelised Apple Pâté

The complexity of Cragganmore 12 year old lends itself to many dishes, here, its honey, blackberry and stewed fruit notes, perhaps even a hint of apricot create a wonderful background to this delicious chutney.

We've had a bumper crop of rhubarb this year so we have enjoyed many rhubarb puddings, ice creams, jams and chutneys. I love chutney! I have created this one for my cousin and life long friend Mike Beatt who loves the rhubarb and ginger combination. This is a fantastic chutney that you can use as an accompaniment to many dishes from cheeses to pork, lamb, curries, sandwiches and salads. It's my current favourite, I hope it will become yours.

2 kg rhubarb, trimmed and chopped
500g raisins
1 litre distilled white vinegar
900g granulated sugar
2 teaspoons salt
50g stem ginger, finely chopped
2 cloves garlic, crushed
$1/_2$ red chilli, chopped finely
the juice and grated rind from 2 large oranges
60-100mls Cragganmore 12 year old Malt Whisky
1 large pinch ground mace

You will need a preserving pan and 6 or 7 jam jars with lids.

■ Place the rhubarb, raisins and vinegar in the preserving pan and bring to the boil. Now add the sugar, stir in and simmer to dissolve. Add all of the other ingredients and continue to simmer uncovered for about an hour until the chutney thickens and has a jam like consistency. Stir occasionally so that it does not stick. It is ready when you draw the spoon across the bottom of the pan and it leaves a dry channel which takes a second to fill in. Check for taste and add a little more whisky if necessary. Allow it to cool slightly and then spoon into warm, sterilised jam jars. Fill to the brim and seal with a lid. If using waxed discs, they must be applied immediately to form a seal and then the cellophane covers can be attached.

■ Store for 6 weeks before using because it improves with keeping. If kept in a cool, dark, dry environment this chutney will keep for at least a year, probably much longer. Once opened, store in the fridge and eat within a month. Don't forget to label and date your jars. If you use pretty labels you will have a lovely gift for a lucky friend if you can bear to part with it....

Dijon Mustard Sauce

The subtle background of cracked pepper and multiple background notes of Hazelburn 8 year old, create an interesting layer of flavour which adds complexity to this very simple sauce which, when served cold is a great dressing or dip for a steak and when warmed up, it makes a wonderful sauce.

This is a delightful, versatile sauce which is so easy to make. Try it with our Brown Trout in Oatmeal recipe. It works really well with fish; vegetable dishes; pork; steaks; chicken; turkey; veal; even salads, and you can experiment with different whiskies and mustards to further increase its versatility.

150mls sour cream or crème fraîche
$1^1/_2$ tablespoons Dijon mustard
10mls Hazelburn 8 year old Malt Whisky to taste
salt and freshly ground black pepper

■ Mix all the ingredients together and serve separately as a cold accompaniment. Now how easy is that!

Accompaniments & Sauces

Honey and Orange Dressing with Aberfeldy

The almost syrupy, orange liqueur flavour of Aberfeldy 12 year old is perfect with this dressing, but you can ring the changes with Auchentoshan Three Wood, you'll be amazed at the totally different flavour it brings.

This dressing is wonderful with lots of salads but works particularly well with Mackerel served hot or cold or try it with Goats Cheese, just lovely!

This dressing is best when prepared several hours in advance and served at room temp.

2 tablespoons orange juice
1 tablespoon Aberfeldy 12 year old Malt Whisky
1 generous tablespoon honey
2 teaspoon dried thyme
2 tablespoon balsamic vinegar
6 tablespoons olive oil
pinch salt

■ Whisk olive oil, salt, honey, thyme, orange juice and whisky well. Then whisk in the vinegar until well blended.

Laphroaig® Cream Sauce

This is one for the really peaty whisky lovers, Laphroaig 10 year old's unmistakeable flavours are present through all levels of this sauce. It is very easy to make and is great with haggis, chicken and prawns, in fact anything!

125mls beef stock
100mls double cream
15mls Laphroaig 10 year old Malt Whisky
25-50g butter
salt and freshly ground black pepper

■ Place the beef stock in a pan, bring to the boil and reduce by a half. Now add the cream and bring back to the boil. Add the whisky and the butter. Start with 25g butter, whisk it in and taste. Season and add more butter or cream to taste. The longer you cook this sauce the milder the whisky becomes.

Whisky Cumberland Sauce

30mls Glenmorangie 10 year old Malt Whisky
125mls fresh orange juice
2 tablespoons grated orange zest
225g redcurrant jelly, best quality you can find
pinch salt
pinch cayenne

The delicate notes of Glenmorangie 10 year old, some nutty, some herbal and just a slight floral hint create the most amazing layer to this quickie sauce. It is a very easy version of Cumberland Sauce, delicious with gammon, pork pies, game dishes and vegetable pies.

■ In a medium saucepan, combine the whisky, orange juice, and orange zest, and bring to a boil. Lower the heat and simmer, stirring occasionally, until reduced by a half. Add the redcurrant jelly, salt, and cayenne, and stir well. Allow to cool before serving. This sauce will keep well in a sealed container in the fridge for 2 weeks.

Blue Cheese Sauce

Glenmorangie 10 year old contributes its delicately nutty, herbal and lightly spiced flavours to this versatile sauce.

This is a very rich, flavoursome sauce that you can use in lots of dishes from steaks to vegetables. You can also make it in advance and reheat it when you require it.

■ Pour the white wine into a pan and bring to the boil and reduce it to about a half, add the whisky and stock and reduce again to about a half, add the blue cheese. Stir and allow it to begin to melt then add the double cream, bring up to the boil, stirring occasionally, taste and season with salt and pepper.

■ It is now ready to serve with beef steaks; pork; chicken; turkey; mussels; pasta and vegetables like cauliflower, broccoli and potatoes. Try it, it is fabulous!

Serves 4

225mls dry white wine
50mls Glenmorangie 10 year old Malt Whisky
300mls stock, beef, chicken or vegetable
50g Strathdon blue cheese
100mls double cream
a little salt and freshly ground black pepper

Dark Vegetable Stock

This is a very useful, flavoursome stock which you can use when you don't want a specific meat flavour and of course it is suitable for vegetarians.

■ Place all the ingredients into a large pan and bring to the boil, simmer gently for an hour. Set aside overnight, or for several hours (if possible), to cool and allow the flavours and colour to develop. Strain into a bowl or jug and it is ready for use.

■ For a **Light Vegetable Stock** just omit the mushrooms and if you wish, it will be ready for use as soon as it is cooked.

■ Clean vegetable peelings, water that vegetables have been cooked in can all be added to the stock pot, to add flavour. You can vary the flavour of the stock by varying the vegetables you use or the herbs or spices.

Makes about 1 litre

250g mushroom, chopped roughly, including stalks
1 large onion, chopped roughly
the skins from the onions, they add colour
1 carrot, chopped roughly
1 stalk of celery, chopped roughly
1/2 leek, cleaned and chopped in half
1 clove of garlic
2 bay leaves
6 black peppercorns
1 teaspoon white wine vinegar
1 pinch thyme
1.5 litres water

Apple, Rosehip and Glen Moray Jelly

- Photographed with Venison and Pork Terrine

Glen Moray 16 year old's barley sugar, boiled sweetie background notes create an interesting layer of taste in this versatile accompaniment.

In the late summer early autumn the wild rose bushes in the hedgerows are laden with beautiful plump red rosehips and are there for the picking, but be careful the stems are very prickly. Wear long sleeves! This recipe can happily vary according to the amount of rosehips you pick. Rosehips are very good for you as they are full of Vitamin C and the jelly is lovely spread on toast or on freshly baked scones, but a spoonful at the side of a pork or game terrine is also delightful. You can even add it to a pork gravy to give it an unusual lift. It is so tasty, I'm sure you will find lots of other ways to use it.

■ Wash the apples and cut into quarters, place in a large preserving pan add the rosehips and just cover with water. Boil the fruit until soft, and pulpy.

■ Scald the jelly bag with boiling water and suspend it over a bowl. Pour in the fruit pulp and liquid.

■ Allow this to drip overnight. Do not be tempted to squeeze the bag or the resultant jelly will be cloudy.

■ The following day, measure the juice in the bowl and allowing 1lb sugar for every pint of juice, pour the juice into the preserving pan and stir in the sugar over a moderate heat until all the sugar dissolves.

Stirring continuously, bring to the boil and boil rapidly for about 10 minutes, removing any scum that forms.

■ Check to see if the jelly will set by dropping a little on to a cold plate and after a couple of minutes tip the plate slightly and see if the jelly wrinkles. If it does it has reached setting point.

■ Once this point is reached, remove from the heat and allow the jelly to cool for a few minutes. Add 30mls whisky. You can vary the amount according to your taste. Pour the jelly carefully into warm, sterilised jars avoiding creating air bubbles.

■ Cover, label and store for 3 months before using. *(if you can wait that long....)*

3kg cooking apples

1¹/₂ kg washed rosehips (you can use any amount up to half the weight of the apples)

water, sufficient to cover the fruit

granulated sugar (quantity depends amount of juice extracted)

30mls Glen Moray 16 year old Malt Whisky (or to suit personal taste)

You will need a large jelly pan (preserving pan) & jelly bag.

Buttery Whisky Sauce

This is a yummy butter sauce similar to brandy butter and so it is wonderful with Christmas Pudding but it is also lovely with Queen of Puddings (page 158), Bread and Butter Pudding and lots of others. Try it with your favourite pud.

■ Combine sugar, water and butter in saucepan and cook until dissolved. Remove from heat and add whisky to your taste, heat through and serve. Simmering it longer will fade the taste of the whisky.

Serves 4-6

125g sugar
60mls water
60g butter
10-20mls to taste of a whisky of your choice, for example BenRiach would work well with Christmas Pudding and Aberfeldy or Cragganmore with Queen of Puddings

Spiced Whisky Custard Sauce

This is a lovely version of crème anglais, perfect for Christmas Pudding, Fruit Pies and Christmas Pies.

■ Put the milk, cream, cinnamon stick with the vanilla seeds and pod in a pan low heat and slowly bring to the boil. Remove from the heat and set aside for 30 minutes so that the flavours can develop. Meanwhile whisk the egg yolks, whisky, cornflour and sugar in a bowl until the mixture has thickened and is a pale yellow colour. Remove the vanilla pod and the cinnamon stick and bring the milk mixture back to the boil.

■ Add one ladleful of the hot milk to the egg mixture and mix in using a wooden spoon. Then stirring constantly, add the egg mixture back into the pan with the remaining milk mixture. Stir the mixture constantly over medium-low heat until the mixture is the consistency of heavy cream and coats the back of the wooden spoon. If using vanilla extract add it now. Because we have added a little cornflour this sauce will be stable and you will be able to reheat it when you need it.

Serves 4-6

150mls full cream milk
150mls single cream
1 stick of cinnamon
1 vanilla pod, split and the seeds scraped out (or 1 teaspoon vanilla extract)
3 large free range egg yolks
50mls BenRiach 15 year old Dark Rum Wood Malt Whisky to taste
1 teaspoon cornflour
25g caster sugar

Variation

Chocolate Custard Sauce

■ This is a gorgeous chocolaty custard which will go well with steamed and baked puddings.
■ Follow the recipe above, omit the cinnamon stick and melt 25g grated dark chocolate or chocolate chips in the milk when it is warming.

Orange Butterscotch Sauce

This is a very useful sauce which you can serve with steamed or baked puddings, baked bananas and ice creams.

Serves 4-6

- See the Steamed Walnut and Prune Pudding Recipe on page 154, follow the Butterscotch Sauce recipe and add the grated rind of ½ orange

Variation
- You can add the grated rind of a small lemon instead of the orange to create yet another delicious sauce.

Chocolate Fudge Sauce

Glenmorangie 10 year old's delicate, nutty and slightly herbal background with its hint of vanilla, provides a very pleasing addition to this sauce.
Amazing on ice cream or served with sponge puddings. *Yum...*

- Place the chocolate in a bowl over hot water, add the butter and allow them to melt, stirring occasionally. Warm the milk slightly and blend it into the chocolate mixture. Transfer to a small saucepan and add the sugar and the syrup. Place over a low heat and stir until the sugar has dissolved. Now bring to the boil and boil steadily for 5 minutes without stirring. Remove from the heat and add the vanilla and the whisky and mix well.
- If you are serving this sauce over ice cream and you want it to harden quickly, boil it for an extra 3 minutes.
- To reheat, place in a bowl over simmering water.

Serves 6-8

50g dark chocolate, at least 60% cocoa solids, broken in pieces or use callets/chips

30g butter

60mls milk

200g soft brown sugar

6 level tablespoons golden syrup

1 teaspoon vanilla extract

10-15mls Glenmorangie 10 year old Malt Whisky

Accompaniments & Sauces

Chocolate Lattice - *Photographed with Double Chocolate Tart*

So many whiskies work well with chocolate and the classic The Macallan 10 year old is no exception. The Macallan Distillery which has an excellent visitor centre is located at Easter Elchies on a hill overlooking the River Spey with magnificent views over to Aberlour and beyond. It is well worth a visit, the whole area is stunning. From the 16th century there are records of our McConachies living and working in this area, and in the grounds of the Distillery we were surprised to find a peaceful little graveyard which is the last resting place of many McConachie ancestors. But I digress, back to the chocolate.... These little lattice shapes will dress up lots of your desserts and cakes. They are a very pretty, useful little addition to your culinary repertoire and The Macallan just gives it that decadent little extra.

90g dark chocolate, chopped small or callets/chips. 60% or more cocoa solids
1 dessertspoon butter
5-10mls The Macallan 10 year old Malt Whisky

▪ Place all the ingredients into a heatproof bowl and melt the chocolate either over a pan of simmering water or gently in the microwave. Stir briskly to ensure all the chocolate is melted and to combine the ingredients.

▪ Now pour the chocolate into a piping bag fitted with a small nozzle. Alternatively use a strong freezer bag and snip a tiny piece off one corner, creating a piping bag.

▪ Place a non stick silpat mat or greaseproof paper on a tray and pipe zig zag lines on it and then pipe more zig zag lines on top, in the opposite direction. Then make as many more as you need and place the tray in the fridge until they set. You can also pipe rosettes and other shapes as you wish.

▪ Now use to decorate ice creams and other desserts. Looks especially good with the Chocolate Chip Columba Ice Cream (page 196), but you could also serve them with Chocolate Mousses (page 182), Double Chocolate Tarts (page 184), Double Chocolate Drambuie Dreams (page 164) and I'm sure you can find lots of other excuses to use them.

Variation
▪ Use white chocolate buttons, add the whisky but not the butter and continue as above.

Whisky stills at Balvenie Distillery

Lowland Region

The Lowland malt whisky region embraces the mainland of Scotland south of an imaginary line drawn between Dundee and Greenock, and includes the cities of Edinburgh and Glasgow, extending south to the Cheviot Hills bordering England. Grain whisky, which is used as a base for blended whiskies, is mostly produced in the south of this region.

There was a time during the mid 19th century when every sizeable town in the Lowlands had its own distillery, supplying the English market as well as local demands. In terms of overall style, Lowland malt whisky is much lighter than the Highland style, with little or no peat used in the malting of the barley, resulting in a much broader appeal. These days with modern distillation techniques it is easier to source Highland malts with a light character to suit the requirements of blenders, so there are now only 3 operating malt distilleries in the lowland region.

Entering the Lowlands from the south west and taking a left turn into Dumfries and Galloway, you can stand at Scotland's most southerly point, breathing the fresh sea air as you look out at Ireland, England and the Isle of Man silhouetted against the setting sun. Having taken in the breathtaking view, you can head back towards Gatehouse of Fleet and The Cream o' Galloway Visitor Centre at Rainton Farm.

Rainton Farm has been managed by the Finlay family since 1927 and since 2001, has enjoyed full organic status. In 1994 they established The Cream o' Galloway Dairy Company and began making quality ice cream and frozen yogurt with milk from their own dairy. They currently produce over 200,000 litres of ice cream a year in over thirty flavours as well as a range of Organic Fairtrade frozen smoothies. The visitor centre offers over four miles of fully accessible nature trails and an adventure playground, so that both children and adults can get some exercise after being cooped up in the car.

Moving north into Ayrshire you enter Burns Country and no visit to the Lowlands is complete without the Robert Burns experience. Scotland's national poet, penned over 500 works, including some of the world's best known poems and songs, so a visit to The Burns National Heritage Park at Alloway and the simple clay cottage where the poet was born is a must. The cottage is now fully restored to its original condition and the visit is enhanced with audio-visual interpretations bringing the childhood world of Robert Burns to life.

Now heading north east into Lanarkshire you will find yourself in the rolling hills of the southern uplands where the production of cheese has been a focus of pastoral life for centuries. Humphrey Errington's farm at Walston Braehead near Carnwath is helping to keep this tradition alive. Both Lanark Blue and Lanark White are made from the milk of his flock of 400 ewes; additionally he makes Dunsyre Blue from the milk of Ayrshire cows. The recipes Humphrey uses are as old as the surrounding hills and the quality of his cheese lays testament to his devotion to his art. Widely available throughout Scotland, Braehead cheeses adorn traditional Scottish cheeseboards in many of the country's top restaurants.

From Carnwath you can travel to Glasgow or Edinburgh. These two cities have had more tour guides written about them than any other place in Scotland, so we will concentrate on the whisky. A must when visiting Edinburgh is the Scotch Whisky Heritage Centre next to Edinburgh Castle. Even the kids will enjoy learning about Scotch whisky as they join you on the whisky barrel ride - a journey through the history of whisky production over the last 300 years. Many of the famous names that shaped the development of the Scotch whisky industry are represented on the tour and you may even learn some of the secrets of whisky blending from the ghost of the Master Blender.

Heading north west out of the capital takes you to Falkirk, the home of one of the most spectacular engineering and design wonders of the modern age. The Falkirk Wheel is the centrepiece of the UK's largest canal restoration project and as the world's only rotating boat lift, it has reconnected the Union Canal with the Forth & Clyde Canal and re-established east to west coast boating. It is a great place to spend the day, walking around the modern visitor centre or just standing and marvelling as you watch the rotation of the wheel raising and lowering boats the 24 metre distance between the two canals.

To the east of Edinburgh along the A1 lies East Linton just outside Dunbar. Here you'll find Knowes Farm Shop, which is part of a family farming business producing and selling its own eggs, potatoes, vegetables and herbs.

The shop also stocks wonderful home made soups, preserves, pâtés and puddings. The Cochran family are fiercely local in their sourcing policy and the shop also sells a wide range of fish, game, venison, poultry, cheese, ice cream, dairy produce, honey, duck and quail eggs. Well worth a visit to stock up the larder if you are self catering.

At the far north east of the lowland region we find Dundee, this friendly city has gone through a number of phases of reinvention over the years. Now known as the City of Discovery it is the home of the RRS Discovery, Captain Scott's Antarctic exploration vessel built in Dundee and now a 5 star visitor attraction. The city enjoys a dramatic setting on the River Tay, one of the world's most beautiful estuaries, it is dominated by Dundee Law, an extinct volcano around which Dundee was built some 800 years ago. A visit to the top of the Law provides a great vantage point to see for miles in all directions. Facing west you can see Balgay Hill with its Observatory and then along the beautiful Tay valley towards Perth; facing south are the Tay Bridges leading across the silvery Tay to the lovely villages of north Fife and the Lomond Hills and then to the north there's the Sidlaw Hills which shelter Dundee from the worst excesses of Scottish weather. On the eastern outskirts of Dundee you come to the beaches of Broughty Ferry, Monifieth and Carnoustie where Sheila and her family spent many happy summers. Dundee has an enviable reputation for its music concerts and of course its famous Repertory Theatre, the only theatre in the UK with a resident company. There are living museums offering fascinating glimpses into our industrial past; castles to visit; a lake with water sports at Camperdown Country Park; numerous excellent golf courses in addition to the championship courses of nearby St Andrews and Carnoustie; so with lots of possible sporting activities and cultural opportunities, there is plenty to enjoy for all the family.

Baked Nectarines with Glayva™, Ginger and Pecans

Glayva's sweet, honey, spicy background and citrus notes blend superbly with the sweet fruit and spicy filling in this scrumptious dessert.
This gorgeous dessert is so easy to prepare but it looks beautiful and is packed full of flavour. The Glayva creates a wonderful syrupy sauce.

Preheat oven to 200°C/Gas 6

■ Halve and stone the nectarines, lightly scoop out the cavity using a melon baller (or very carefully with a teaspoon) and place the nectarines skin side down on a baking tray.

■ Crush the biscuits by placing them in a polythene bag and rolling over it with a rolling pin, empty into a bowl and set aside. Chop the pecans, reserve a teaspoonful for garnishing the plates and mix the remainder with the crushed biscuits, the melted butter, honey, orange rind and the egg yolk. When combined spoon the mixture into the cavities in the centre of the nectarines.

■ Pour the orange juice, water and Glayva around the nectarines and bake for 20 minutes until the filling is lightly browned and the nectarines are cooked. *You can prepare to this stage earlier in the day and reheat when you want to serve them.*

To Serve

■ Place three half nectarines on each plate with a heaped spoonful of crème fraîche beside them, then spoon some of the delicious syrup from the baking tray around the fruit. Top the crème fraîche with a sprig of mint and sprinkle the reserved chopped pecans decoratively around the plate and enjoy......

Variations

■ I love this with crème fraîche because it balances the sweetness of the honey and the Glayva but it is also lovely with vanilla ice cream. This recipe also works well with peaches, but you need to remove the skins, so cover the halved peaches in boiling water, leave for 30 seconds and the skins come off easily, then proceed as above. You can also use your own choice of nuts, for example toasted almonds are wonderful sprinkled on top of the stuffing and pistachios bring a whole different flavour.

■ Then of course you can use amaretti biscuits instead of the gingernuts, there are lots of delicious alternatives but I'm sure you will want to keep the Glayva....... *mmm.....Cheers!*

Serves 4

6 large nectarines

Stuffing
4 gingernut biscuits
50g pecans
30g butter, melted
2 teaspoons clear honey
finely grated rind of 1 orange
1 egg yolk

Sauce
juice of one orange
75-90mls Glayva
50mls water

Garnish
240g crème fraîche
4 sprigs of mint

Steamed Walnut and Prune Puddings with Butterscotch Sauce

BenRiach 15 year old Dark Rum Wood's rich rum soaked fruit background marries perfectly with this light yet fruity pudding.

These delicious little puddings are based on the walnut puddings I made at school in Dundee, rather a long time ago. I have added whisky soaked prunes which make the puddings juicy and soft and I have laced the butterscotch sauce with whisky which it certainly wasn't at school.... You will love these, I promise....

Preheat oven to 180°C/Gas 4

▪ Start by roughly chopping the prunes and then place them in a bowl with the whisky and leave to soak.

Now lightly grease the pudding basins and set aside. Cut greaseproof paper into 6 pieces about twice the size as the top of the pudding basins, grease them lightly and make a fold in the form of a pleat down the centre. Now set them aside and start to make the puddings.

▪ Begin by creaming the butter and sugar together until it is light and fluffy then whisk in the eggs a little at a time. Sift the flour with the baking powder and carefully fold it in to the mixture. Now add the chopped nuts, coffee essence and prunes with any liquid and stir to combine.

▪ Divide the mixture between the 6 pudding basins which should be two thirds full. Now place the greaseproof lids on the puddings, twisting the edges of the paper under to seal the lids. The pleat in the middle will allow the puddings to rise. To ensure that the lids stay on you can tie a piece of string around the neck of the basins on top of the paper, or you could use an elastic band. Place the puddings in the pan and pour boiling water in to come about half way up the pudding basins. Place a lid on the pan and allow it to boil gently for 45 minutes. Check the water level and top it up if necessary.

▪ Meanwhile, make the Butterscotch Sauce. Place the sugar, syrup and butter into a pan, melt together then boil for 1 minute. Allow the mixture to cool slightly then add the whisky and milk and beat it in until well combined.

▪ After 45 minutes switch off the heat and remove the lid, taking care not to get scalded. After a few minutes, take the puddings out of the pan, remove the lids and allow the puddings to cool slightly before loosening them from the sides of the basins. Shake the puddings and pat the bottom of the basins ,then when they feel loose in the basins, turn them out on to your serving plates. Place half a walnut on top of each pudding and pour the butterscotch sauce over the top. Serve with a scoop of Vanilla Ice Cream and enjoy....

Variation

▪ I have steamed these puddings because they are moister and lighter when steamed, but if you have less time you could bake them, they are still delicious. Use exactly the same recipe but don't cover them. Place them on a baking tray and bake for 20 minutes at 180C/Gas 4.

Serves 6

Puddings

60g ready to eat stoned prunes

15mls BenRiach 15 year old Dark Rum Wood Malt Whisky

125g softened butter or soft buttery margarine

125g caster sugar

2 eggs, whisked

150g plain flour

1 teaspoon baking powder

50g walnuts, roughly chopped, plus 6 half walnuts for decoration

2 teaspoons coffee essence

Butterscotch Sauce

120g soft brown sugar

2 dessertspoon golden syrup

120g unsalted butter

10-15mls BenRiach 15 year old Dark Rum Wood Malt Whisky

2 tablespoons milk

You will need 6 pudding basins or ramekins and a large pan to act as a steamer.

Spiced Fruit Compote

BenRiach Dark Rum Wood is a wonderful match for any fruity recipe and it lends a lovely Caribbean background note to this dish.
This compote has all the glorious scents of Christmas and it has the added advantage of being delightfully healthy.

■ There are 3 methods of cooking this dish. Long slow roasting in the oven for 3 hours which is fabulous, cooking in a saucepan for 20-30 minutes which is lovely or cooking in the microwave for about 5 minutes.

■ This is the quick method. Combine all the ingredients except the seeds in a bowl and place in the microwave on high heat for about 5 minutes depending on the wattage of your microwave. Check and stir after 2 minutes. If the fruit absorbs all of the juices, add a little more orange juice and continue cooking. It is ready when the fruits are plump and the juices are sticky. Allow to sit for a few minutes then remove the lemon peel, cinnamon sticks and cloves. Sprinkle in the seeds and you are ready to serve.

To Serve

■ Delicious served warm over ice cream with little shortbread biscuits. It is equally wonderful served with crème fraîche or mascarpone, whichever appeals to you. Alternatively, it makes an incredible breakfast dish especially in the festive season.

500g pack of mixed dried fruits
100g dried cranberries or cherries if you can find them
25mls BenRiach Dark Rum Wood 15 year old Malt Whisky
the peel of 1 lemon
the juice of half a lemon
1 cinnamon stick
4 cloves
the juice of 4 oranges
15mls balsamic vinegar

Garnish
100g sunflower seeds or your favourite seeds

Rhubarb Queen of Puddings

The sweet nose and complex body of Aberfeldy 12 year old provide a delicious link between the crumble and whisky cream.

We think this impressive retro pudding is due a comeback. Here we have taken it to a new level by adding a spoonful of whisky infused rhubarb and ginger as an additional layer.

Preheat oven to 180/Gas 4

▪ Bring the milk to boiling point and add the breadcrumbs, butter, sugar and ground ginger. Stir together then leave for 20 minutes to cool and to allow breadcrumbs to swell.

▪ Meanwhile, chop the rhubarb into small chunks and cook gently with the sugar, whisky and chopped ginger until the rhubarb is just collapsing, remove from the heat and place a spoonful of cooked rhubarb in the bottom of each ramekin.

▪ Next whisk the well-beaten egg yolks into the breadcrumb mixture and pour into the phased ramekins. Place them on a baking tray and bake in the oven at180C/Gas 4 for about 25 minutes until set.*

To Serve

Preheat oven to 190-200C/Gas 5-6

▪ Whisk the egg whites until stiff, add the caster sugar and whisk again. It should be thick and glossy. Spoon the meringue on top of the puddings, sprinkle with chopped glacé cherries and bake until set and the meringue is lightly browned. This will take 5-10 minutes.

▪ If kept warm they will keep for several minutes then you can serve them with a jug of cream or even more special, Cragganmore Honeyed Cream. (see page 187)

*You can make these puddings to this stage, cover them and place them in the fridge where they will keep for up to a week. You will need to warm them slightly before you finish them with the meringue.

575mls full cream milk

110g white breadcrumbs

25g butter

60g caster sugar

1 teaspoon ground ginger

2 or 3 sticks young rhubarb

25g sugar

15mls Aberfeldy 12 year old Malt Whisky

1 piece stem ginger in syrup, chopped quite small

3 eggs separated, keep the egg whites for the meringue

2 extra egg whites

150g caster sugar

3 glace cherries, chopped

You will need 6 buttered ramekins or individual oven proof dishes. These puddings also look wonderful in glass dishes because you can then see the layers.

Bruléed Figs with Whisky and Mascarpone

The mellow flavour and malty sweetness of Cardhu Single Malt Whisky combine exceptionally well with the honey and sweet figs. This simple but very glamorous dessert is just that little bit different and would be lovely on the Christmas table. Deliciously impressive!

Serves 4

■ First make the tuilles (page 166), make them as long as your serving dishes.

■ Place the honey and whisky in a pan and bring to the boil, stirring all the time. Cut figs in half lengthwise and drizzle each one with some of the honey and whisky mixture, reserving the remainder. Let the figs sit for at least 5 minutes to absorb the mixture then pat dry with a paper towel. Sprinkle with demerara sugar and brulée with a kitchen blow torch or place under a very hot grill until the sugar caramelises.

To Serve

■ Mix the mascarpone with enough double cream to loosen it, stir in the orange zest, juice and the reserved whisky and honey mixture and pour some on the base of each serving plate. Place 2 half figs in the centre, drizzle a little chocolate sauce into the mascarpone sauce and serve with a twisty tuille on each plate.

30mls heather honey
30mls Cardhu Single Malt Whisky
8 large ripe figs
25g demerara sugar
200mls mascarpone
50mls double cream
zest of 1 orange plus 4 teaspoons orange juice
small quantity chocolate sauce (see page 148 or good quality shop bought)
long twisty tuilles (page 166)

Desserts and Sweeties

Pineapple and Coconut Upside-Down Pudding

In this pudding the pineapple is marinated in the wonderful, rummy flavoured BenRiach whose spicy, citrus finish complements the coconut, spices and lime flavours in the pudding.
Jamaica meets Scotland in this delicious updated retro pudding.

Preheat oven to180C/Gas 4
Grease the 4 individual pudding basins or ramekins

■ First place 4 pineapple rings in a saucepan with 2 tablespoons of the reserved juice and 30mls whisky, bring to the boil and simmer for a couple of minutes and then set aside. Reserve the remainder of the pineapple juice for the coulis.

■ Make the topping by warming the syrup and whisky in a saucepan or microwave. Pour a little into the bottom of each pudding basin. Place the pineapple rings on top and a cherry in the centre of the rings.

■ Sieve the flour, baking powder, salt, ginger and cinnamon into a large bowl, add the coconut, mix well and set aside.

■ Now cream the butter and sugar until light and fluffy, add the zest and juice of 1 lime then whisk in the egg a little at a time. Carefully fold the dry ingredients into the mixture. If necessary, add enough milk to a dropping consistency. Finally, spoon the mixture over the pineapples and pour about ½ teaspoon of whisky on top of each. Place the pudding basins on a baking tray and bake in lower half of oven for approximately 40 minutes or until risen, set and golden brown.

■ Meanwhile make the coulis. In a small saucepan, add the marinade juices, the remaining pineapple juice, the lime juice and zest and cook until syrupy. You may need to add a little water and sugar if you have insufficient syrup.

■ Allow the puddings to cool slightly, then run a knife around the sides and turn them out on to the serving plates. Dress the plate with the fruity coulis and serve with a dollop of crème fraîche or a scoop of vanilla ice cream on the side.

Serves 4

Marinade
1 small can pineapple rings in natural juice, drained and the juices reserved
30mls BenRiach Dark Rum Wood
15 year old Malt Whisky

Topping
100mls golden syrup
15mls BenRiach Dark Rum Wood
15 year old Malt Whisky
6 glacé cherries

Pudding
90g plain flour
½ teaspoon baking powder
1 pinch salt
½ teaspoon ground ginger
½ teaspoon ground cinnamon
25g dessicated coconut
90g butter, softened
90g soft brown sugar
1 lime, zest and juice
2 medium free range eggs, beaten
25mls milk or as necessary to make a dropping consistency

Coulis
reserved marinade
reserved pineapple juice
1 lime, zest and juice

You will need 4 individual pudding basins or ramekins (or 1 x 8" diameter, deep cake tin).

Desserts and Sweeties

Double Chocolate Drambuie® Dreams

This pretty Drambuie flavoured dessert combines rich dark chocolate and luscious white chocolate custards to create a luxurious ending to a meal; perfect for chocoholics everywhere.

Ideally, you should start this recipe the day before. You can either make one then the other or have fun with two pans at the same time. The method is the same regardless.

▪ To start, heat the milk and cream in a pan then add the chocolate and stir frequently until the chocolate is melted. Now whisk together the egg yolks, sugar, cornflour and Drambuie (plus cocoa for the dark chocolate version).

▪ Add the melted chocolate, stir well and return the mixture to the pan. Cook over a gentle to medium heat, stirring all the time until the custard is thick enough to coat the back of a wooden spoon. Now allow it to cool in the fridge for at least 8 hours to allow it to set.

To Serve
This looks lovely in a pretty wine glass

▪ Spoon enough white chocolate custard carefully into each glass to 2/3 fill then equally carefully top with the dark chocolate. *(Do not totally fill the glass)* Place back in the fridge until you are ready to serve them.

▪ This is delightful with a Scotch Whisky Snap (see recipe on page 194) or a thin shortbread biscuit.

You can reverse the colours and top the white chocolate custard with shavings of dark chocolate.

Serves 6-8

White Chocolate Dream
300ml / ¹/₂ pint milk
300ml / ¹/₂ pint double cream
175g white chocolate, broken into small pieces
4 egg yolks
50g golden caster sugar
2 teaspoon cornflour
30mls Drambuie (or to taste)

Dark Chocolate Dream
As above but with only 1 teaspoon cornflour and the addition of 1 teaspoon cocoa powder

Glen Moray Chocolate Truffle Torte

Served with Raspberry Coulis and a Basket of Scottish Summer Fruits

Glen Moray 16 year old has a boiled sweetie taste and a long complex finish which will not be drowned by the chocolate.

This dish was Graham's award winning dessert at the Spirit of Speyside Chef of the Year 2007 Competition and, despite the long list of ingredients, is not difficult to recreate.

Serves 8-10

Lightly oil ten 8 cm mousse rings (4 cm high).

▪ *Tip: If doing this for a dinner party send the old man out to the hardware store and buy a length of 3 inch drainpipe, cut this into 4cm lengths, put them through the dishwasher and you have got a bag full of mousse rings for the cost of 2 stainless steel ones.*

▪ Place the mousse rings on a tray covered with cling film. Mix the butter, nuts and digestive biscuits with the whisky and divide the biscuit base between all ten, press the mixture down with the back of a spoon and then place the tray in a refrigerator.

▪ Now break up the chocolate and place in a heatproof bowl with the golden syrup and about 150ml of the cream. Place the bowl over a pan of hot water (not touching the water) leave on a medium heat for 15 minutes or until the chocolate has melted. (or alternatively, place in the microwave for about 20-40 seconds, depends on how powerful your microwave is.) Remove from the heat and stir to combine the ingredients. Set aside until cooled slightly.

▪ Add the remaining ingredients to a large bowl, whisk until the cream leaves a trail for a second or two. Do not over whisk otherwise when you mix in the chocolate the mixture may seize.

▪ Pour the chocolate mixture over the whipped cream and combine with a large spoon until the mixture is evenly coloured. Do not worry if the mixture seems runny it will thicken more as you stir. Now divide the mixture between the mousse rings and smooth the tops with a palate knife and refrigerate for 2¹/₂ - 3 hours until set.

Raspberry Coulis

▪ Place the caster sugar and water in a small pan, bring it to the boil and simmer until a syrupy texture is achieved. Add the raspberries and lemon juice and bring back to the boil, simmer until the raspberries have broken down and the coulis thickens. Pass through a fine sieve and refrigerate.

Tuille Basket

▪ Cream the butter with an electric whisk then add the remaining ingredients and combine to form a thick batter.

Torte

6 digestive biscuits, crushed

2 heaped tablespoons chopped mixed nuts

50g soft unsalted butter

25ml Glen Moray 16 year old Malt Whisky

vegetable oil for greasing mousse rings

250g dark chocolate (minimum 60-70% cocoa solids)

2 tablespoons golden syrup

568ml double cream

4 teaspoons instant coffee granules

1 teaspoon ground cinnamon

25 ml Glen Moray 16 year old Malt Whisky

Coulis

100g caster sugar

100ml water

250g raspberries

1 squirt lemon juice

Tuilles Baskets

120g plain flour

120g icing sugar

4 egg whites

1 pinch salt

50g unsalted butter

Garnishes

Selection of fresh summer fruits, enough to fill eight small tuille baskets

icing sugar for dusting

Glen Moray Chocolate Truffle Torte (continued)

- Place in a piping bag and pipe narrow lines onto a non stick oven tray.
- Place a teaspoon of the mixture per person onto another non stick oven tray and smooth out with the back of the spoon to form a disc, this will form the fruit baskets.
- Place on the top shelf of a preheated (180 C/Gas5) oven for 5 minutes until golden brown.
- Remove the strips of tuille and spiral round a wooden spoon or knife steel. Work quickly but gently, as the tuilles will set very quickly and become very brittle. Allow to cool.
- Set the discs over the base of a small glass (or use an egg!!) and shape gently but quickly into baskets, set aside and allow to cool *(if you find that the tuilles become cold and crisp you have finished shaping them, don't worry, just pop them back in the oven for a few seconds to soften, and start again).*

To Serve
- Trickle a little of the coulis decoratively on to each plate.
- Place the torte in its ring on a fish slice this will make the setting out easier. To remove the tortes from the rings, heat gently with a kitchen blow torch or wrap with a hot tea towel until you see the chocolate starting to melt around the edges, lift off the ring.
- Gently slide the torte off the slice into position on the plate.
- Garnish with the tuille basket filled with fresh summer fruits dusted with a little icing sugar and decorate the torte with the tuille spiral.

Your guests will be so impressed!

Teacher's® Spiced Lemon and Ginger Creams

Teacher's Blended Scotch Whisky, a widely available blend, has a lovely citrus rind finish that complements this unusual creamy dessert very well, providing a cleansing flavour through every mouthful.

This pretty dessert looks so rich but it is actually very light. It manages to be creamy yet fresh and spicy, a perfect finale for a dinner party.

Serves 4

■ Put all of the ingredients except the cream and egg whites into a bowl stir well and then leave the mixture to stand for at least 15 minutes. Now stir the cream slowly into the whisky mixture until evenly blended, and then beat with an electric whisk or rotary beater until thick. Beat the egg whites until stiff peaks, and then fold them into the cream mixture until blended in, taking care not to lose the air.

■ Spoon into 4 pretty wine glasses or sundae dishes then chill in the refrigerator for at least 30 minutes.

To Serve

■ Serve chilled topped with a trickle of ginger syrup and a little lemon zest, with Scotch Whisky Snaps (page 194) on the side (don't fill them with cream). How beautiful is that?

You can make this dessert a couple of hours in advance but not much longer or the egg whites will separate within the mixture.

60mls Teacher's Blended Scotch Whisky

2 tablespoons lemon marmalade

grated zest of 1 lemon, save a little for the garnish

juice of one lemon

2 pieces of stem ginger in syrup, chopped quite small, about 1 dessertspoonful

2 teaspoonfuls lemon grass purée

6 cardamon pods, split and the seeds removed and ground finely (in a pestle and mortar if you have one, if not tip them into a bowl and grind them with the end of your rolling pin)

2 tablespoons caster sugar

250mls double cream, chilled

2 egg whites

ginger syrup for topping

Glen Moray Lacy Chocolate Baskets

So many of the Speyside malts work very well with chocolate so it is difficult to choose any one, however, Glen Moray 16 year old's sweetness and hint of cinnamon provide an interesting yet subtle layer to these useful little baskets.

We already know that chocolate and whisky works and the mixing of orange and chocolate has long been accepted as a classic match so this makes the perfect threesome for these pretty baskets which make a very glamorous dessert, but are actually very easy to make.

Makes 8-10

Preheat oven to 180C/Gas 4

■ Lightly grease a large baking tray or use a non-stick mat. Melt the butter with the syrup, grated orange rind and sugar gently in a small pan, stirring until the sugar is dissolved and the mixture is combined. Now stir in the flour and cocoa mixture and mix until smooth. Finally add the whisky and mix it in well.

■ Place dessertspoonfuls of the mixture a few inches apart on the baking tray and bake for 6-8 minutes until they spread to thin lacy circles and begin to turn a little darker at the edges.

■ While they bake, turn your chosen glasses or egg cups upside down on your work surface.

■ Once they are baked, leave them to cool slightly, but whilst still warm, working 2 at a time, lift the biscuits from the tray, lay over the bases of the glasses and press into soft folds with your fingers. Now, working quickly, make the rest of the baskets. *Don't worry if they don't look perfect, that adds to their charm.*

■ If they become too cool, place the tray back in oven for a few seconds to soften them a little.

■ If they are not required immediately, allow them to cool completely and store in a cool place in an airtight container.

50g butter
50g golden syrup
grated rind of 1 orange
150g golden caster sugar
50g plain flour sifted with
15g cocoa powder
20mls Glen Moray 16 year old Malt Whisky

You will need 2 small based glasses or egg cups.

To Serve

■ These pretty lacy baskets can be filled with a scoop of well chilled Chocolate Mousse (page 182), Ice Cream (page 196) or even a few seasonal fruits and a little coulis or icing sugar.

Ginger Plum Puddings

For a long time Longmorn Malt Whisky was a hidden Speyside secret, now the 16 year old is widely available and much sought after. This malt offers spice, toffee and honey on the nose, with butter and more spice on the palate and more dry spice in the finish, all in all the perfect match for this pudding.

A delicious retro pudding brought bang up to date with Longmorn Malt Whisky, it is very gingery and the Longmorn soaked plums make it quite luscious.

Preheat oven to180C/Gas 4

Grease 4 individual ramekins and line with cling film (or 1 x 8" diameter, deep cake tin).

▪ Place the plums, sugar, and the whisky in a saucepan with the water if you need it, and bring to a simmer and cook until the plums are softened then set aside.

▪ Brush the cling film inside the ramekins, lightly with oil. For the sauce, place the butter, sugar and whisky in a small pan to melt, whisk it together and spoon a little over the base of the ramekins and place 2 plum halves on top, cut side up.

▪ Place a roasting pan in the bottom of the oven and half fill with boiling water to provide steam for the puddings and especially for the cling film.

▪ Sieve the flour, bicarbonate of soda, salt, ginger and cinnamon into a large bowl, add the chopped ginger and set aside. Heat the butter, sugar and treacle in the microwave or saucepan until the butter has just melted. Do not allow it to boil. Remove from the heat, stir in the milk and egg and then stir it into the dry ingredients and beat well to combine. Spoon the mixture on top of the plums, trickle about a teaspoonful of whisky on top and place the ramekins on a baking tray and bake in the centre of the oven for 40-50 minutes or until set and golden brown. Allow to cool slightly before turning out on to the serving plates.

To Serve

▪ Lovely with a dollop of chilled Crème Fraîche, a scoop of Sorbet or Vanilla Ice cream.

Variations

▪ We have made individual puddings but you could make one family sized one. You could also vary the fruit, pears also work very well with the ginger and Longmorn.

Serves 4

Topping

30mls Longmorn 16 year old Malt Whisky

4 fresh plums, stoned

10g soft brown sugar

20mls water, if the plums are not ripe

Sauce

30g unsalted butter

50g soft brown sugar

10mls Longmorn 16 year old Malt Whisky

Pudding

90g plain flour

$1/2$ teaspoon bicarbonate of soda

1 pinch salt

$1/2$ teaspoon ground ginger

$1/2$ teaspoon ground cinnamon

25g crystallised stem ginger or chopped stem ginger in syrup

45g butter

60g soft brown sugar

60g black treacle

75mls milk

1 small egg, beaten

Pine Kernel Toffee Tart

This is a delicious luxurious tart which takes a traditional French recipe from Provence and enhances it with Glen Moray 16 year old. The Auld Alliance is alive and well!

Serves 8-10

Vanilla Pastry

125g butter, softened

125g sugar

1 vanilla pod, split and the seeds scraped out

1 pinch of salt

4 egg yolks, lightly beaten

250g plain flour, sieved

Filling

100g sugar

100g butter, chopped into small chunks

400g pine kernels

30mls Glen Moray 16 year old Malt Whisky

30mls double cream

You will need a 21cm loose bottomed tart tin, greased; baking paper and baking beans.

■ Make the pastry first. Mix together the butter, sugar, vanilla seeds and salt and beat until pale coloured and fluffy. Gradually add the egg yolks then fold in the flour a little at a time. Do not beat. Now turn out on to floured board, bring it all together, place in a polythene bag and refrigerate, ideally for 4 hours.

Preheat oven to 200C/Gas 6

■ Bring the pastry dough out of the fridge and allow it to come to room temperature before continuing.

■ Roll out the pastry to fit your tart tin. Line the greased tin with the pastry then line the pastry with baking paper and fill with baking beans. Place the tin on a baking tray and bake for about 15 minutes (baking blind). Remove the paper and beans from the tart and return the pastry to the oven for a few minutes to set the pastry. It will be going back in the oven later so it doesn't have to be fully cooked at this stage..

Reduce oven temperature to 160C/Gas 3

■ Before you begin to make the caramel, make sure you have everything ready to go - the butter and the cream next to the pan, ready to put in. Making caramel is a fast process that cannot wait for hunting around for ingredients. If you don't work fast, the sugar will burn.

■ Heat the sugar on a high heat in a large heavy bottomed pan. As the sugar begins to melt, stir constantly with a whisk. As soon as all of the sugar crystals have melted and the liquid sugar is medium dark amber in colour, quickly add the butter to the pan. Continue to whisk vigorously until the butter has melted.

■ Now add the pine kernels, stir in and take the pan off the heat. After a moment or two add the whisky and the cream to the pan and continue to stir to incorporate. Handle the mixture with care because it is extremely hot. Put back on the heat for a minute or two and stir until the toffee is combined with the pine kernels.

■ Pour the mixture into the pastry case and return it to the oven for a further 20 minutes. Set aside to cool, remove from the tart tin and serve cold with a scoop of vanilla ice cream. *Magnifique!*

Basket of Roasted Fruits

We make no apologies for using Glayva again here. It is so delicious and utterly perfect for this dish. This colourful dessert of roasted fresh fruits is wonderful at the end of a filling meal and you can use whatever fruits you have available.

The fruit in this dish must be cooked very quickly so that they remain firm..

■ To start, mix the Glayva, honey, cinnamon and orange juice together and set aside.

■ Heat the butter and oil in a large frying pan while you prepare the fruit. Chop the bananas into fairly large chunks cut on a diagonal, core and slice the apple, keeping it quite chunky. Chop each plum in half, removing the stones and place in the pan with the bananas, apple and rosemary, allow the fruit to brown on one side and add the physalis and grapes. Turn the fruit to brown on the other side and then add the brambles and strawberries, toss briefly in the hot pan and add the Glayva mixture. Keep the heat up high and when it is all combined remove the rosemary and serve immediately in a tuille basket with a scoop of vanilla ice cream or crème fraîche on the side.

Variations

■ Of course you can use other fruits like nectarines, peaches, pears, blueberries and pineapple, and you can also very easily adapt this dish to make it suitable for vegans. Use vegan margarine or just sunflower oil, omit the honey and serve with soya ice cream....*truly delicious!*

Serves 4

60mls Glayva
2 teaspoons honey
½ teaspoon cinnamon
50mls orange juice
1 sprig rosemary
25g butter and a little sunflower oil
2 firm bananas
1 apple
4 physalis, if you can find them in your greengrocer's
2 plums
12 grapes
8 brambles (blackberries)
8 strawberries

Tuille Baskets

For these delightful baskets see the Chocolate Truffle Torte recipe (page 178) and make them larger by shaping over the base of a tea or coffee cup

The DramBrulée

Drambuie with its honeyed spicy flavour gives a wonderful Scottish twist to the classic Crème Brulée. Absolutely wonderful!

This is another dish that you can prepare well in advance, leaving you free to enjoy the company of your guests. This recipe will make either 5 or 6 portions depending on the size of your dishes. This is a very easy but impressive dessert to make. Enjoy!

Preheat oven to 145C/Gas 1¹/₂

■ Whisk the egg yolks with the castor sugar until pale, add the cream, milk and Drambuie and leave mixture to rest for 1 or 2 hours to infuse with the flavour of the Drambuie.

■ Pour into the glass dishes and bake in a bain marie for 1¹/₄ hours or until set but still a little wobbly in the centre.

■ Set aside to chill and completely set. *You can make the brulées to this stage several hours or even a few days in advance, just cover them and place them in the fridge until you want to serve them.*

■ Then sprinkle the top evenly with a thin layer of sugar, making sure that all of the custard is covered. Now switch on your blow torch and play the tip of the flame over the sugar until it is all melted and golden brown. Try not to burn the sugar or boil the custard!

■ If you don't have a blow torch, switch your grill on to its highest heat and allow it time to heat up. Now place the brulées on to an ovenproof tray and set under the grill as close to the heat as possible. Watch carefully so that the sugar does not burn.

■ The sugar topping is very hot at this stage so allow the brulées a few minutes to cool and for the sugar to set. The topping should now be crisp and they are ready to serve.

To Serve
Garnish with some fresh fruit on the side or in a tuille basket (page 166).

*Create a bain marie using a deep roasting tin, place the brulées in it. Put the tin in the oven and then pour boiling water in to come half way up the glasses. This is easier and safer than adding the water before it goes in the oven.

Makes 5-6

6 egg yolks
50g castor sugar
200mls double cream
150mls milk
50mls Drambuie
6 teaspoons demerara sugar for the brulée topping (or caster or granulated sugar)

Garnish
fresh fruit to serve

You will need a large roasting tin to act as a bain marie* and 6 pretty ovenproof glass dishes, shallow brulée dishes or ramekins. Also, ideally, a kitchen blow torch.

Chocolate and Orange Mousse

On the nose, Arran 10 year old offers citrus notes, figs and toffee, its background notes of spices, nuts and vanilla balance the creamy chocolate and create a subtle layer of flavours which turn this simple dessert into something very special indeed! A little bit of chocolate heaven!

Serves 4

■ To start, place the chocolate with the whisky and grated orange rind in a heatproof bowl over a pan of simmering water. Turn off the heat and leave until it is melted. Set aside.

■ While the chocolate is melting, make the sugar syrup. Place the sugar and water together in a pan and bring to the boil, simmer until it thickens to a syrupy consistency. Set aside.

■ Whisk the egg yolks lightly in a large bowl. Pour the sugar syrup into the egg yolks whisking all the time with an electric whisk or rotary beater. Continue whisking until the mixture becomes pale and thick.

■ Now lightly whip the cream to soft peaks texture and carefully fold the cream into the chocolate mixture using a metal spoon until it is well blended. Place in the fridge to chill. *(You can make the mousse to this stage 2 or 3 days in advance).*

120g dark chocolate, (minimum 60% cocoa solids) broken or use callets/chips

50mls Arran 10 year old Malt Whisky

grated rind of 1 orange

100mls water plus 100g caster sugar for sugar syrup

4 large free range egg yolks (save the whites for making meringues)

250mls double cream

To Serve

■ Spoon into pretty glasses and refrigerate to chill and set then serve decorated with whipped cream and white or dark chocolate curls with a Scotch Whisky Snap on the side (page 194).

Variation

■ Chill until scoopable and serve in Glen Moray Lacy Chocolate Baskets. (page 172).

Desserts and Sweeties

Double Chocolate Tart

This luscious tart is a dream to make and a dream to eat. You will make your guests very happy people with this creamy dessert! The dark chocolate pastry crust contrasts wonderfully with the creamy white chocolate filling which has been enlivened by the lovely rummy flavoured BenRiach.

Preheat oven to 200C/Gas 7

■ First make the pastry. Sieve the flour, cocoa powder and icing sugar together. Add the butter and rub in using your finger tips until the mixture resembles fine breadcrumbs. Now in a small bowl beat the egg together with the ice cold water and add to the mixture. Cut into the mixture with a knife until it comes together to a soft dough, adding more water if necessary. Do not over work it or you will make it tough. Turn the dough out on to a floured work surface and knead lightly, then cover in cling film and put it in the fridge to chill for 30 minutes until it is firm. Dust the work surface with flour and roll the pastry dough out quite thinly. Use it to line one large tart ring or 6 individual tartlet rings, do not stretch the pastry or it will shrink back when it is baked. Now line the tin(s) with greaseproof paper, pile in some baking beans and place on a baking tray, then bake blind for 6-8 minutes for the individual tartlets and 20 minutes for the large one, until the pastry is set but not browned. Remove the baking beans and put the tart case(s) back in the oven for a further 5-10 minutes until crisp. Set aside to cool then carefully remove from the tins. Return them to their tins to provide support when you fill them.

■ Meanwhile make the white chocolate filling. Put the white chocolate in a heatproof bowl and place the bowl over a pan of simmering water until the chocolate collapses. The bowl must not touch the water or the chocolate will seize and it will be ruined. When the chocolate melts remove it from the heat, stir it ensuring that there are no lumps then mix in the double cream and the whisky until it is all combined. It should be smooth and fairly thick. Set aside to cool a little and then spoon into the pastry cases and level the tops.

■ When you are ready to serve, top with fresh fruit. Make a glaze by heating the redcurrant jelly in a small pan with 3 tablespoons water and stirring until smooth, pour a little of the warm glaze over the berries, dress the plate with strawberry coulis and chocolate lattice (page 149) or a little chocolate sauce and serve.

Serves 6

Chocolate Pastry
200g plain flour

25g cocoa powder

50g icing sugar

100g cold unsalted butter, cut into small pieces

1 large egg yolk

4 tablespoons ice cold water

Filling
300g white chocolate, broken into pieces (or use butons, callets or chips)

200mls double cream

15mls BenRiach 15 year old Dark Rum Wood Malt Whisky

Topping
vary this with whatever soft fruit is available

350g fresh strawberries

100g fresh blueberries

6 large raspberries or brambles (blackberries)

200g redcurrant jelly

3 tablespoon water

You will need one 25cm loose bottomed tart case or six individual loose bottomed tartlet cases 10cm in diameter. You will also need dried beans, rice or ceramic baking beans for baking the pastry blind.

Scotch Plum and Ginger Crumble

A wonderful tasty oaty crumble made even more exciting by the addition of Cragganmore 12 year old which enhances the fruity orange flavour, making the most amazing juices.
You can serve this simply with custard, pouring cream or even more wonderful, a Cragganmore™ Honeyed Cream mmm......

Preheat oven to 200C/Gas 6

- Start by cutting the plums into quarters and remove the stones then place the plums in an ovenproof dish. Next add all of the remaining filling ingredients and stir into the plums. The aroma is now glorious......
- The next step is to rub the butter into the flour until the mixture resembles fine breadcrumbs and then add the remaining topping ingredients. Sprinkle the topping over the plums and place the dish on a baking tray and bake for about 30 minutes or until golden brown. The plums will be cooked but not totally collapsed and there will be lots of gorgeous juice. How easy is that!
- Serve with Cragganmore honeyed cream, custard or pouring cream.

Cragganmore™ Honeyed Cream
- Whisk all the ingredients lightly together until just beginning to thicken. Check for sweetness and add more honey and or whisky to taste.
- Pour around each portion of Crumble and enjoy.....

Variation
- This recipe is also delicious with rhubarb instead of plums.

Filling
1 kilo plums
90mls Cragganmore 12 year old Malt Whisky
grated rind of 1 orange
120g demerara sugar
1 teaspoon ground ginger

Crumble Topping
180g plain flour, sifted
90g butter
90g caster sugar
1 teaspoon ground ginger
60g porage oats

Cragganmore™ Honeyed Cream
285mls double cream
15mls Cragganmore 12 year old Malt Whisky
15mls runny honey

Tipsy Laird

Drambuie is such a versatile liqueur that works so well in desserts that we could not leave it out of this celebratory Scottish Trifle. This trifle was always served in our home whenever we had anything to celebrate from birthdays, through weddings and homecomings to Christmases and New Year. It wasn't always laced with alcohol of course and there were usually "hundreds and thousands" and silver balls on top! Drambuie makes a wonderful addition to the Sherry because it is magic with raspberries and with cream. I hope that you will enjoy it as much as we do.

Serves 6-8

■ Spread raspberry jam on the slices of trifle sponge, put one on top of the other and cut into pieces. Now place them in the base of a large glass bowl. Mix the Drambuie with the Sherry, (mmm, smells wonderful...) stab the sponges with a fork and then sprinkle the alcohol evenly over the sponge allowing it to soak in. Next add a layer of raspberries and sliced bananas. Set aside while you make the custard.

■ To make the custard, whisk the egg yolks with the sugar and vanilla extract until pale and creamy. Heat the milk and cream in a pan until it reaches boiling point then stir it into the egg mixture. Once it is well blended, return the mixture to the pan and stir continuously over a low heat until the custard thickens. Do not boil or it will split. Pour it into a dish and cover so that a skin doesn't form, set aside to cool.

■ When quite cool, pour the custard over the layer of fruit, spreading it evenly. Next whip the double cream, whisk in the Drambuie to taste, add sugar to sweeten if necessary and spoon on top of custard. Decorate with toasted almonds and sliced bananas and a few strands of orange peel and it is ready to serve.

5 trifle sponges, cut in half (alternatively, 8-10 sponge fingers or 1 small Victoria sponge)

300g raspberry jam, home made or good quality

50mls Drambuie

50mls Sherry

250g raspberries

1 large banana

Custard

2 egg yolks

50g castor sugar

a few drops of vanilla extract

250mls milk

150mls double cream

Topping

500mls double cream

5-10mls Drambuie

1 tablespoon castor sugar to taste

a few toasted almonds, about 1 teaspoonful

1 medium/large banana, sliced and dipped in a little lemon juice, to garnish

a few fine strands of orange peel to garnish

My Mum's Canadian Tart with Scotch

I have no idea what is Canadian about this tart but I do know that it was a big favourite in our Dundee household, and then much later I always had to have one baked for when my son Jamie came home from University. I have tweaked it a bit by soaking the dried fruit in Aberlour a'bunadh. My Mum Ada, would have been thrilled to see that I have included her recipe. You can serve this cold with a cup of tea or coffee or warm with a dollop of Aberlour cream as a dessert.

Serves 8-12

Preheat oven to 190C/Gas 5

- Place the dried fruit in a bowl with the whisky and set aside until you have everything else ready.
- Now make the pastry. Sieve the flour and salt into a bowl. Rub in the butter until a breadcrumb texture is achieved. Now cutting into the mixture with a knife, add the egg yolk and cold water gradually, cutting and turning until it comes together to a soft dough, adding more water if necessary. Do not over work it or you will make it tough. Turn the dough out on to a floured work surface and knead very lightly, cover in cling film and put it in the fridge to chill for 30 minutes. It is really important to allow the dough to rest at this stage, otherwise it will be very difficult to roll and it will break and crack, ultimately making it heavy.
- Roll the pastry out larger than the size of your tart case and lift it using the rolling pin, carefully ease it into the tin, do not stretch it or it will shrink back when baked, gently press it on to the base and sides. Cut away any excess so that the edges come slightly above the top edge of the tin then crimp the edges with your fingers or if your tart case is fluted, roll across the top with your rolling pin, so cutting away the excess. Set aside the excess pastry for decorating the top of the tart. Place the tart and the remaining pastry back in the fridge to cool and firm.
- Meanwhile make the filling. Cream the butter and sugar until light and fluffy then gradually add the eggs mixed with vanilla extract, beating well. Don't worry if it curdles. Now add the fruit and stir in. Take the pastry and the tart from the fridge and roll out the remaining pastry and cut with a pastry wheel or sharp knife into 12 x 1cm/½ inch-wide strips, then freeze them on a baking tray for 5 minutes.
- Spoon the filling into the tart and twisting the strips, lay them on top of the filling creating a lattice pattern, pressing the ends onto the edge to attach them. Paint the lattice lightly with an egg glaze and bake for 25-30 minutes until golden brown and set. Allow to cool in the tin for 10 minutes before setting to cool on a wire rack. This cake will keep for about 2 weeks if kept in an airtight tin. *Mine never lasts that long!....*

To Serve
- Dust with icing sugar if you like and serve with the whisky and honey cream.

Short Crust Pastry
225g plain flour
pinch salt
120g butter, cut into small pieces
1 egg yolk
1-2 tablespoon icy cold water

Filling
175g sultanas
175g raisins
75g glace cherries, halved
50mls Aberlour a'bunadh Malt Whisky
100g butter, softened
100g caster sugar
2 large free range eggs, whisked
1 teaspoon vanilla extract
a little whisked egg for an egg wash

Garnish
icing sugar for dusting
100mls Double Cream whisked with 15mls Aberlour a'bunadh Malt Whisky and honey

You will need a 22cm loose bottomed tart case, lightly greased.

Lush Chocolate Cakes with Cherries Aberlour

This is a velvety, soft centred chocolate dessert, influenced by the French Moelleux au Chocolat. They are desserts rather than cakes because they are best served warm. The cherries are fabulous when marinated in the rich cask strength Aberlour a'bunadh, juicy, sweet and luscious.

Serves 4

Preheat oven to 180C/Gas 4

■ Place 12 cherries in a bowl with the whisky and set aside. They can marinate for up to 24 hours.

■ Melt the chocolate and butter in a bowl over a pan of simmering water (or carefully in the microwave) then stir in the whisky. Lightly whisk the egg yolks, add them to the chocolate and mix together. Add the sugar and the flour a spoonful at a time whisking until smooth. Whisk the egg whites until soft peaks, do not over beat. Now a little at a time carefully incorporate the egg whites into the chocolate mixture taking care not to lose the air.

■ Butter the insides of the cake rings and place them on a baking tray lined with a non stick silpat mat or greased greaseproof paper. Butter both sides of strips of greaseproof paper wide enough to line the cake rings and come a further 2cm/1inch above the top. Line the sides with the strips of greaseproof paper. Divide the mixture between the ramekins and place 2 cherries in the centre of each one.* Bake for 15 minutes or until well risen and set. Remove from the oven and allow to cool for 3 minutes in the rings, then turn out on to the plates and serve immediately dusted with sieved cocoa powder or icing sugar.

125g dark chocolate, 60% or more cocoa solids

65g unsalted butter

Aberlour a'bunadh Malt Whisky

3 large free range eggs, separated

125g caster sugar

30g plain flour, sifted

pinch of salt

12 morello cherries (bottled)

You will need 4 cake rings or ramekins.

you can prepare to this stage earlier in the day and bake at the last minute because they only take 15 minutes in the oven.

To Serve

■ With a scoop of vanilla ice cream and a little chocolate sauce. *Enjoy!*

Desserts and Sweeties

Scotch Whisky Snaps

Aberlour a'bunadh is a cask strength malt that has a punch that matches its 60% alcohol content. That being said it has a wonderfully spicy, sherried background with a hint of nuts and raisins. These snaps are absolutely fabulous and very versatile because you can serve them in traditional fashion, stuffed with cream with a nice cup of tea or coffee, but they are delicious on their own served with Ice Creams (page 196); Mousses (page 182); Double Chocolate Drambuie Dreams (page 164) or Teacher's Spiced Lemon and Ginger Creams (page 170) and I'm sure you will find lots of other excuses to serve them.

Preheat oven to 180C/Gas 4

■ To start, lightly grease 2 baking trays or use a tray with a non stick baking mat.

■ Melt the butter with the syrup and sugar gently in a small pan, stirring until the sugar is dissolved and the mixture is combined. Now add the lemon juice and remove from the heat. Stir in the flour and ginger mixture and mix until smooth, then add the whisky and mix well.

■ Drop teaspoonfuls of the mixture a few inches apart on the baking tray and bake for 6 – 8 minutes until lacy and golden brown. They spread a lot during cooking so don't put too many on each tray. When beginning to cool but still warm, remove from the tray with a palette knife and wrap around the handle of a thick wooden spoon. Allow them to firm before removing them, then working quickly, make the rest of the snaps. If they become too cool, place the tray back in the oven for a few seconds to soften them a little.

■ *If not required immediately, allow to fully cool and store in an airtight container in a cool dry place where they will keep for a few weeks if you can stop yourself or your family eating them.......*

■ Just before serving, whip the cream and pipe it into each end of the whisky snaps.

50g butter

50g golden syrup

50g demerara sugar

1 teaspoon lemon juice

50g plain flour, sifted with

1 teaspoon ground ginger

1 teaspoon Aberlour a'bunadh Malt Whisky

140ml double cream

Glayva™ and Mango Ice Cream

This is a heavenly ice cream with a gorgeous rich colour. The Glayva complements the mango, adding spice and honey flavours. This is a quick and easy ice cream recipe, you don't need to make a custard or own an ice cream maker and it is still scrummy!

▨ Ideally using an electric beater, whip the cream and milk until it starts to thicken, add the condensed milk and beat in. Now add the mango pulp and the Glayva and continue to beat until it reaches the consistency of softly whipped cream. Pour into a freezer proof box and freeze for 12-24 hours. It will now be ready to scoop and serve. You could serve it with a Nutty Praline to add texture or in a Glen Moray Lacy Chocolate Basket (page 172) with slices of fresh mango on the side. *Scrumptious!*

500mls double cream
125mls milk
450ml tin condensed milk
450g mango pulp, tinned is fine
120mls Glayva, this is the maximum quantity or it will not freeze properly

Variations
▨ This ice cream can be poured into cling film lined individual moulds and then frozen. Alternatively, pour into a lined terrine and cut it in slices to serve. Try adding chopped fresh mango or chopped stem ginger.

Chocolate Chip Columba Cream

This is a rich, dreamy, chocolaty ice cream with a fabulous kick. Very, very special! It is also made using the same easy method as the Glayva and Mango Ice Cream. If you like chocolate you will love this one!

▨ Follow the method as above, stirring in the chocolate pieces at the end.
▨ Serve as it is with a little chocolate sauce on the plate or in a Tuille Basket (page 166) or a Glen Moray Lacy Chocolate Basket (page 172).

500mls double cream
125mls milk
450ml tin condensed milk
150mls Columba Cream Liqueur
50g dark chocolate, chopped fairly small (60-70% cocoa solids)

Desserts and Sweeties

Aberlour Panna Cotta with Raspberries

Panna cotta is Italian for cooked cream. It is a fabulously light dessert and in our version it is flavoured with Aberlour heather honey and the wonderful Aberlour a'bunadh. The raspberries and shortbread biscuits continue the Scottish theme. We are so lucky here in Scotland to have the most wonderful soft fruit in the world so we try to make the most of them when they are in season. We also love Aberlour Heather Honey, so when you visit Aberlour which I highly recommend, don't go home without a jar of John Wilson's Heather Honey.

Serves 6

■ Start by making the panna cotta. In a saucepan bring the cream and milk to the boil, reduce the heat and simmer for 5 minutes and remove from the heat. Meanwhile soak the gelatine in cold water for about 5 minutes until soft. Squeeze out any excess water from the gelatine then stir in to the milk and cream along with the honey and whisky. Stir well until the gelatine is dissolved, bring to a simmer and then strain into a jug, fill the moulds and leave to cool to room temperature. Cover and place them on a tray and chill for at least 4 hours or until set. You could make these the day before and store in the fridge until you are ready to serve them.

■ Meanwhile make the raspberry coulis (page 166) and set aside.

■ For the raspberry glaze, pulp the raspberries by pressing them through a sieve then place the pulp in a saucepan with the sugar. Bring to the boil rapidly for a few minutes and skim any scum off the surface. Pour into a bowl, cover with cling film and allow to cool.

■ Toss the remaining raspberries in the glaze.

To Serve

■ Place serving plate on top of panna cotta and turn them upside down, holding tightly together, give a firm shake or two to loosen. If they don't come out, dip the moulds briefly into some hot water to loosen the panna cotta and then turn it out as above, top with a few glazed raspberries and surround by raspberry coulis. Serve with little shortbread biscuits see Balvenie Shortbread page 215. *mmm.... absolutely delightful!*

Varation

■ The recipe also works well with powdered gelatine or Vege-Gel vegetarian gelatine alternative, but make sure you follow the instructions on the packet.

Panna Cotta
6g gelatine leaves, 2-3 leaves dependent on their size
400 ml double cream
100 ml milk
2 tablespoons heather honey
2 tablespoons Aberlour a'bunadh Malt Whisky

Glaze
100g raspberries
30-40g caster sugar

Raspberry Coulis
100g caster sugar
100ml water
250g raspberries
2 teaspoons lemon juice

Garnish
15-20 raspberries

You will need 6 moulds or ramekins.

Auchentoshan® Pecan Chocolate Truffles

The mellowness of the Auchentoshan Three Wood Malt Whisky and the nutty, spicy overtones complement the chocolate and the pecans perfectly and the chocolate cake crumbs make these little gems decadently rich and very chocolaty!
A very luxurious truffle to have with coffee at the end of a wonderful meal. They also make a lovely gift when placed in petit four cases and packed in a pretty box or bag tied with a ribbon. You will have very happy friends!

Makes 36

- First grind the pecans coarsely in a food processor and add the chocolate cake, process briefly and empty into a large bowl. Now mix in the sugar, syrup, and whisky very thoroughly. This is much easier with your hands.
- Next, take teaspoonfuls of the mixture and roll and shape the mixture into balls then roll them in caster sugar or cocoa powder. I usually make some of each. Place them on a tray covered in greaseproof paper and put the tray in the fridge until the truffles are set firm. Box them in an airtight container and keep in a cool place.
- Alternatively, freeze them on a baking sheet until each one is firm and then store them in a freezer proof container.

125g pecans
150g chocolate cake crumbs
175g icing sugar
1 tablespoon golden syrup
30mls Auchentoshan Three Wood Malt Whisky
caster sugar and/or cocoa powder for rolling and dusting

Variations

- This recipe also works well with chocolate biscuits instead of the cake. In that case, process the biscuits with the pecans then follow the recipe above.
- You can also vary the nuts of course, walnuts work very well, just choose your favourite and enjoy them.
- A different whisky will also give you another variation. See the notes on page 216 for ideas as to which whiskies will match these ingredients.

Scotch Chocolate Crunch

250g non dairy margarine
4 tablespoons golden syrup
2 dessertspoons cocoa
4 dessertspoons non dairy drinking chocolate
45mls Dalwhinnie 15 year old Malt Whisky
200g raisins
500g digestive biscuits, crushed roughly. (check the packet to make sure that they are vegan)
200g plain vegan chocolate

Dalwhinnie 15 year old has distinct wild flower notes and a honey sweet background that match every ingredient in this delightful petit four.

This no bake biscuit is delicious and so quick and easy to make! It is a very useful recipe to have in your repertoire to delight your friends who do not, or cannot eat dairy. It freezes beautifully and is best served direct from the freezer.

You will need a lightly greased Swiss Roll Tin 28cm x 18cm.

▪ Melt everything except the biscuits and chocolate gently in a large pan. Remove from the heat, add the raisins and crushed biscuits and mix well. Scrape the mixture into a greased baking tray and press down firmly with your hand.
▪ Melt the chocolate, pour over the top of the cake and spread evenly with a palette knife. Place in the fridge for one hour to set, then cut into slices and serve........mmm!

Variations
▪ Try this recipe with ginger or tea biscuits or choose your favourite and create your own speciality. This is delicious as it is but of course you could make it non vegan if you wanted to.

Teacher's® Highland Tablet

My Dad's Nippy Sweetie

500mls milk
225g butter
1.8kg caster sugar
400g sweetened condensed milk
45mls Teacher's Blended Scotch Whisky

You will need a greased Swiss Roll Tin 28cm x 18cm.

The finishing citrus notes of Teacher's Blended Scotch Whisky provide a sharp contrast to this buttery tablet.

Tablet is a delicious, buttery, extremely sweet, traditional Scottish sweetie which has been made in Scotland since the early 1800s. It is similar to fudge but harder and grainier. I've created this recipe in honour of my Dad, who called whisky "a nippy sweetie" and made the best tablet I ever tasted. However, he never thought of adding a dram of whisky to it, I think he would have loved this!

▪ Place the milk and butter in a heavy based saucepan on a low heat and melt the butter. Add the sugar and bring to the boil, stirring all the time. Once it is boiling add the condensed milk and boil for 20 minutes. Again keep stirring to avoid sticking or burning. You will know it is ready when it thickens and the colour changes and becomes a light tan colour.
▪ Remove from the heat and beat vigorously for 5 minutes, adding whisky to taste. It will gradually become grainy just continue beating and scraping the sides of the pan and incorporating the crystals into the mixture.
▪ Pour into the greased tin and allow it to cool a little, then score with a sharp knife while it is still soft. Once it has cooled, cut into bars or small squares. The texture is crumbly and melt-in-the-mouth.
▪ Once properly cold, tablet will keep for weeks in an airtight box or will make a lovely gift when packed into a pretty jar.

Desserts and Sweeties

Islay and the Islands

There are over 95 inhabited islands around the Scottish coastline. The Scots, more than any other nation in the union, can certainly live up to the claim of being an island race. Like the Highland region, it is the rugged landscapes and wide variation of climactic conditions which lead to the wonderful array of whiskies produced on the islands. Generally, island whiskies are peatier than their mainland counterparts, occasionally with a hint of sea spray on the nose and a smoky background. The legendary Islay malts have a justified reputation for their heavy peatiness and often exhibit more than a hint of seaweed on the palate.

One of the southernmost islands is Arran. Often referred to as a miniature model of Scotland, the north is rugged and hilly whilst the south of the island benefits from a milder climate and is home to most of its residents. The north is less populated but Lochranza is well worth a visit. The village is very picturesque, lying under the shadow of the castle which was once Robert the Bruce's hunting lodge. Then there is The Isle of Arran Distillery, the island's only distillery which opened in 1995, 150 years after the closure of the last "legal" distillery on the island. It has an excellent visitor centre which is a 'must see' before hopping on the ferry to Kintyre.

Although Kintyre is a peninsula not an island, it is worth pausing on your journey to the western islands to explore this lovely area. With only three distilleries, Campbeltown is Scotland's smallest whisky producing region. Characteristically the malts are deep flavoured and full bodied, Glen Scotia has a hint of sea spray about it, whilst Springbank exhibits a deeply raisin scented nose that reminds one of a rich Christmas pudding. Back on your island trail, the ferry from Tarbert arrives in Port Ellen

Having explored the beaches of the twin bays of Port Ellen, take the new road to Bowmore where the white houses arranged in a grid pattern, dominated by the round church present a very pretty sight as you approach the islands administrative capital. Here you will find the first legal distillery on Islay, the Bowmore distillery which today stands tall as a producer of one of the big Islay malts. The view from the headland to the south is no less inspiring, there are stunning views of Northern Ireland reminding one of the close Celtic links between the people of both countries. With no less than eight working distilleries it might be worth scheduling a stop for a night or two on Islay, so that you can make the most of your visit. The established Islay distilleries sit on the shore with their feet literally in the water; it is

perhaps this, combined with the sea air that contributes to the classic flavours of these historic malts.

Looking north from Islay across the half mile wide stretch of water known as the Sound of Islay, the distinctive mountains the 'Paps of Jura' rise out of the skyline. Jura (Deer Island), famous for its remarkable silence and peace is just 30 miles long and 9 miles wide. It only has one road so there is little chance of getting lost on this leg of your journey. With only 180 people and over 5000 deer, Jura is the least densely populated of the Scottish islands, however it does have its own distillery. The deep amber gold colour of Jura malt invites the taster to sample its rich nose, elegant palate and ever so slightly smoky finish, before heading back to catch the ferry to Oban and then onwards to Mull.

Mull is one of our favourite islands; the single track roads slow the pace and seem to make the island larger than it really is. Rugged mountains, warm welcoming villages and castles - especially Torosay castle and gardens, all make the trip to Mull worthwhile. Tobermoray is the main town of the island, and its brightly painted houses curve around the harbour, making it one of the prettiest villages in the islands. Also nestling on the edge of the harbour is the town's distillery, a tour of which takes in its charmingly eclectic range of buildings and a most unusual mash tun. To reach the Isle of Skye from here you must take the road north and then the ferry back to the mainland followed by either the Skye ferry out of Mallaig or via the road bridge at Kyleakin. The bridge would be our preferred option as the view of the Cuillin Hills over the Kyle of Lochalsh is worth the extended drive.

Whichever way you travel to Skye, you will be amazed by the rugged landscapes and the shoreline that has been shaped and reshaped by the power of wind and tide over thousands of years. Southern Skye has no mountains to boast of, however there can be no stranger sight than the palm trees lining the pavement in Ord or the exotic trees in the garden at Armadale Castle. The central region, dominated by the Cuillins, is home to most of the island's larger settlements and the largest, Broadford, is another picturesque island town with modern facilities in a colourful harbour setting. Carbost is the home of the Talisker distillery which produces smooth well proportioned malts with a big peppery kick.

The north of the island is dotted with wee villages, hamlets and dramatic landscapes that have inspired Skye's

Strawberries

arts and crafts movement, which in turn has given rise to many galleries, potteries and local craft outlets, which are all worth a visit. Skye offers such a range of pursuits you will probably want to stay awhile to take it all in. Whatever the time of year, the vibrant colours of the rocks and the ever changing hues of the heather, the jagged mountain outcrops and the views of the mainland, all make Skye a very special place. Leaving the majesty of Skye behind, head back over the bridge and north through Wester Ross to Ullapool and take yet another ferry, this time to the Western Isles.

The islands of Lewis, Harris and the Uists form the Western Isles or Outer Hebrides as they are sometimes known. The stark landscape of Lewis clearly illustrates the harsh lifestyle of its former inhabitants and the museum at Blackhouse will give the visitor a true insight into the way of life of the crofters of yesteryear. Ancient stone monuments abound and for those with an archaeological bent, the 4000 year old standing stones at Calanish will provide hours of interest and fun figuring out what it all means. Heading south the landscape changes and becomes more mountainous, this is a sign that you are nearing Harris. High mountains and deep sea lochs, green heather and white beaches punctuated by grey rocky outcrops give Harris a character all of its own. Tarbert is the largest town on Harris and centres around the ferry port and small harbour. One sound piece of advice. Sunday observance is strictly adhered to on the islands, so if you intend to arrive at the weekend you should plan ahead to ensure that whatever you are hoping to visit will be open and that transport links are operating.

Having navigated your way through some of the islands of the west coast, no Scottish island trip would be complete without a visit to the Orkney and Shetland Isles. Those of you who thought that Scotland ended at John O'Groats could not be more wrong. After centuries of Norse rule, the continuing strong ties between these northern isles and their Scandinavian neighbours are evident wherever you look. Even older links with the past are present at many of the well preserved archaeological sites scattered about the islands. Kirkwall, the capital of Orkney has a medieval street pattern which reveals attractive retail outlets and places of interest with every turn. Enjoy the impromptu traditional music sessions in lots of the bars and take a tour of the fascinating Highland Park Distillery. The thirty or so buildings which make up the distillery, centre around a picturesque courtyard and make walking down the narrow lane to it like entering a wee 19th century highland village, whose only output is whisky.

Lying further north than southern Greenland and Moscow and nearer to Norway than Aberdeen, are the 100 islands that form the archipelago of Shetland. Well blessed with modern transport links, just about every corner of Shetland is accessible to the visitor. Rich in thousands of years of nautical heritage and like Orkney, dotted with ancient monuments, Shetland is a dream to visit. If you brave the January weather, you will witness the festival of "Up Helly Aa". This is a celebration of Shetland's history and a demonstration of the islanders' skills and spirit. It lasts only one day and culminates in the ceremonial burning of the dragon galley. Thankfully the following day is a local holiday, because the celebrations go on and on. The islanders' welcome is always warm and personal, and because commercial tourism has never taken off in any big way, it is this individual welcome that will form an everlasting and charming memory of the islands.

All of the Scottish islands boast their own individual character. From the cultural ties with Ireland in the south to the seafaring Norse links of the far north, the islanders are fiercely individual yet warmly welcoming. Whichever of the islands you choose to visit, you can be assured of a warm welcome and the chance to experience their rich cultural heritage for yourselves.

Lowland Region

Whisky Soda Bread

The distinct spice, and sweet yet dry, undertones of Glenkinchie 10 year old lend a tasty layer of flavour to this classic soda bread, especially when married with scrambled eggs and smoked salmon for breakfast.

This version of soda bread is such a quick, easy way to make a lovely fresh, crusty loaf and is beautifully scented by Glenkinchie. It needs to be eaten the day you make it, but I'm sure that will not be a problem.... However, if there is any left, it is wonderful toasted the following day.

Baking time 30-40 minutes

Preheat Oven 190C/Gas 5

Grease and flour a baking tray and set aside. Now sieve the dry ingredients together, adding the bran from the sieved wholemeal flour back into the mix and stir in.

Beat the egg, whisky and yoghurt together and pour into the dry ingredients. Mix together to make a soft and sticky dough. Now on a lightly floured surface, knead the dough for a few minutes until it is smooth then shape the dough into a round, about 5cm / 2inches deep. Transfer it to your baking sheet. Cut a cross shape on the top of the dough with a sharp knife and bake for 30-40 minutes or until golden brown.

Transfer to a cooling rack and leave to cool.

Lovely with soup and fantastic toasted with scrambled eggs topped with smoked salmon.

Also try serving it with pâtés, terrines, cheese or just with butter and marmalade for breakfast.

300g wholemeal flour (whole wheat)

300g plain flour

2 teaspoons baking powder

1 teaspoon bicarbonate of soda

50g caster sugar

1 teaspoon salt

1 egg, beaten

60-75mls Glenkinchie 10 year old Malt Whisky

375mls natural yoghurt

Banana, Dalmore™ and Honey Teabread

The richly elegant and harmonious flavour of Dalmore 12 year old, coupled with its unique banana notes and very lemony finish shine through this tasty teabread.
Heather honey gives this loaf a wonderful scent and flavour and the Dalmore Malt Whisky adds to the taste explosion. This Teabread is moist and very, very moreish.....

Preheat oven to 180C/Gas 4

To start, lightly grease and line the base and sides of a loaf tin with greaseproof paper then lightly grease the paper.

Sieve the flour and nutmeg into large bowl and rub in the butter until fine breadcrumb texture. Now peel and mash the bananas, add the sugar, lemon rind, eggs, honey and whisky and stir in. Next stir this mixture into the flour mixture. Beat well until evenly combined then spoon this batter into the prepared loaf tin and level the surface with a palette knife or the back of a spoon. Bake for about 1^1/$_4$ hours or until a fine skewer inserted into centre comes out clean.

Towards the end of the cooking time, if the loaf starts to brown too much, cover it loosely with tinfoil. When baked, remove from the oven and allow the loaf to cool slightly in the tin before turning it out on to a wire cooling rack to cool completely.

For the topping, gently warm the honey and whisky in a small pan or in a bowl in the microwave and brush it over the top of the loaf. Sprinkle with the crunchy sugar and leave to set.

Now get the kettle on.......

225g self raising flour
^{1}/$_4$ teaspoon grated nutmeg
110g butter
225g ripe bananas
110g caster sugar
grated rind of 1 lemon
2 large free range eggs, beaten
6 tablespoons thick heather honey
30mls Dalmore Malt Whisky

Topping
2 tablespoons thick heather honey
5mls Dalmore Malt Whisky
rough sugar crystals or demerara or crushed sugar cubes for sprinkling

You will need 1 x 1k loaf tin.

Glenfiddich® Raisin Bread

Make Afternoon Tea go with a swing! This delicious tea bread is stuffed with whisky soaked raisins, oats and orange rind and then served with whisky butter.
Glenfiddich 12 year old is malty and soft. Fruit flavours dominate with a nutty background that give this bread a wonderful aroma and complex taste – try it buttered with a slice of mature cheddar cheese on the side.

Baking time 50-60 minutes

The Raisin Bread

Grease and flour the loaf tin.   *Preheat oven to 180C/Gas 4*

Soak the raisins in Glenfiddich for several hours. If you are in a hurry you can place the bowl of raisins and whisky in the microwave for a minute or two until the raisins are plumped up. Allow to stand while you weigh and prepare the remaining ingredients.

Sieve the dry ingredients, and then add the rolled oats and raisins. Then cream the butter and sugar together until light and fluffy. Now gradually add the egg and beat together until combined. Stir in the orange rind and juice then add the dry ingredients alternately with the buttermilk and mix in until you have a soft dough.

Place the dough in the prepared loaf tin and bake in the oven for 50 minutes – 1 hour, until firm and golden brown.

Turn on to a wire cooling rack and once cooled, cut into fairly thick slices, and serve with the Whisky Butter.

Whisky Butter

Combine the butter and whisky, blending them well. Enjoy!

8 to 10 servings

The Raisin Bread
175g raisins
50mls Glenfiddich 12 year old Malt Whisky
225g plain flour
2 level teaspoons baking powder
$1/2$ level teaspoon baking soda
$1/2$ teaspoon salt
75g rolled oats
50g butter
50g sugar
1egg, beaten
1 tablespoon grated orange rind
juice of 1 orange
275mls buttermilk (lots of supermarkets sell buttermilk now but if you can't get it, use natural yoghurt or sour milk which you can make by adding 1 level teaspoon cream of tartar to 275mls milk)

Whisky Butter
225g butter softened
15mls Glenfiddich12 year old Malt Whisky

You will need a 1kg loaf tin.

Baking

Whisky Dundee Cake

Sometimes you just know when you nose a malt whisky what sort of food it is crying out for and Springbank 10 year old is a classic example of this. It just cries out to be matched with a cake containing currants and raisins – a match made in heaven!

As I am from Dundee, this book would not be complete without a whiskied version of the famous Dundee Cake which is a very pretty fruit cake, often used as a lighter, alternative Christmas Cake. The almond decoration is the distinctive "Dundee" feature, but don't ask me why. This cake is a huge favourite in Rachel and Murray's household, I'm sure it will become yours too.

Baking time 2-2½ hours

Preheat oven to 150C-170C/Gas 2-3

First, soak the peel and the dried fruit in the whisky in a large mixing bowl and set aside.

Lightly grease and double line the base and sides of a loose bottomed cake tin with greaseproof paper, then lightly grease the paper. If you allow the sides of the paper to come about 5cm/2inches above the cake tin the cake will be further protected from the heat of the oven.

Start by creaming the butter and sugar, almond essence, orange and lemon rind together until light and fluffy and then add the beaten eggs very gradually, making sure that each addition is incorporated before adding another.

Mix together the sifted flour, baking powder and mixed spice and gradually fold this into the creamed mixture. Next, stir in the whisky and fruit mixture and the flaked almonds and thoroughly combine, it should now be a soft "dropping" consistency (mixture falls quite easily from a tablespoon), if it is too stiff add a little milk. Now spoon the mixture into the cake tin and spread evenly, make a small depression in the centre and decorate the top with the whole blanched almonds, dipped in a little milk. Arrange in concentric circles, do not press down or they will sink.

Bake for 2-2½ hours, checking after one hour and if top is getting too brown, cover it loosely with foil. Check for "doneness" by pushing a warm skewer into the cake and if it comes out clean it is done. Allow the cake to cool in the tin for about 15 minutes and then turn out on to a wire rack to cool completely.

Store in an airtight tin where it will keep for a week or more. You will find that this cake tastes better if it is kept for a few days before cutting it. That's if you can resist it!

50g chopped mixed peel

50g glace cherries, washed, dried and halved

120g currants

120g raisins

120g sultanas

50mls Springbank 10 year old Malt Whisky

225g butter, softened

225g light brown sugar

grated rind of one orange

grated rind of one lemon

½ teaspoon almond essence

4 large eggs, well beaten

275g well sifted plain flour

1 level teaspoon baking powder

1 teaspoon mixed spice

50g blanched almonds roughly chopped

50g whole blanched almonds, for topping

You will need one 18-20cm/7-8inch loose bottomed cake tin.

Balvenie® Shortbread

The smooth, mellow beautifully combined flavours of Balvenie Doublewood and its nutty, cinnamon spiced background give this orange and ginger shortbread a real lift.
These traditionally Scottish biscuits have been spiced up with orange, ginger and whisky and are of course lovely with a cup of tea or coffee, but if you make thin delicate biscuits they are perfect to serve with ice creams and other desserts.

Baking time 10-15 minutes

Preheat oven to 160C/Gas 3

Cream the butter and sugar with the orange rind and whisky until pale and fluffy.

Chop the ginger very finely and stir in the sifted flours and ginger until combined. Do not overwork the mixture or the biscuits will be heavy. Wrap in cling film and set aside in the fridge for about 10 minutes to chill a little.

Flour your work surface lightly and roll out the biscuit paste to about 1cm thick. Now you can either press the paste into a shortbread mould if you have one and turn out on to a baking tray or you can roll the paste lightly into a strip and cut the shortbread into fingers. I like to roll the paste out very thinly and using a scone cutter or shape cutter, cut into rounds or pretty shapes. Prick gently over the whole surface with a fork, this stops them rising but it also improves their final appearance.

Bake for 10-15 minutes depending on the thickness of the biscuits, until golden brown. Sprinkle with caster sugar while still warm and cool on a cooling rack.

Note: The whisky flavour will be more pronounced in the thicker biscuits.

375g softened butter
125g caster sugar
grated rind of 1 orange
90mls Balvenie 15 year old Malt Whisky
50g Chinese stem ginger, finely chopped
400g plain flour sifted with
125g ground rice, rice flour or semolina

Baking

Scottish Gravadlax

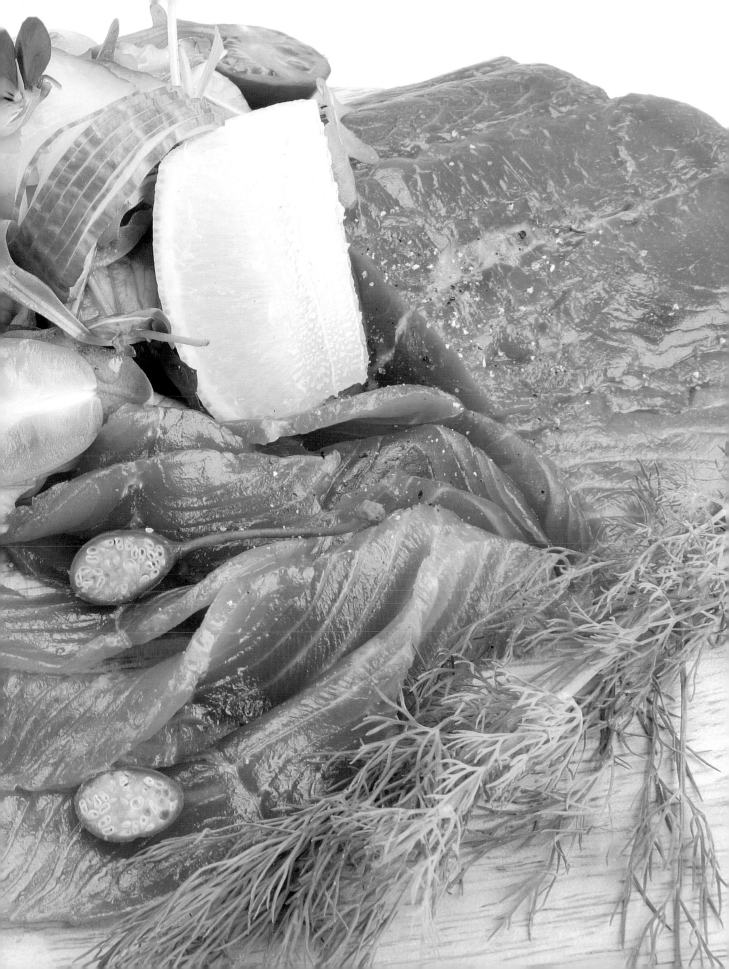

Sourcing Ingredients for Recipes

The power of the internet means that wonderful Scottish produce can be sourced from just about any location in the world. What we have done for you here is to identify some great Scottish producers who sell on line. If you start with the very best ingredients you will be more than half way to creating great dishes to amaze your family and friends. If you cannot buy online or by mail order, always select the very best quality produce available to you locally.

Smoked Salmon from Spey Valley Smokehouse.

The world renowned Spey Valley Smokehouse has been practising the art of curing and smoking salmon for generations using the same age old methods. People from all over the world visit the Smokehouse, deep in the heart of the picturesque Spey Valley. The specialist knowledge of the highly experienced and dedicated team, led by master smoker Jack Wilkinson, is employed to create what we believe is consistently the world's best smoked salmon

www.speyvalleysmokedsalmon.co.uk

Spey Valley Smokehouse, Achnagonalin, Grantown on Spey, Morayshire, Scotland, PH26 3TA.

Tel: + 44 (0) 1479 837078

Naturally Smoked Haddock from Gourmet's Choice.

Gourmet's Choice was founded around 100 years ago by the Great Grandfather of the current owners, and is based in the beautiful fishing village of Portsoy, situated on the Moray Coast in the North East of Scotland. Their smoked haddock is processed using the same techniques as when the company was founded and the result is a pale un-dyed oak smoked product with a distinctive flavour and dependable quality.

www.gourmetschoice.net

Gourmet's Choice, Harbour Head, Shore Street, Portsoy, Aberdeenshire, Scotland, AB45 2RX.

Tel: + 44 (0) 1262 843255

Meat and Game from Stuart Grant Quality Meats.

For 5 generations the Grant family have supplied top quality Scottish meat and meat products to customers throughout Great Britain. Their enviable reputation for quality is well known everywhere from discerning householders to high quality hotels. Scotland is known throughout the world as having the best beef and lamb and Stuart only buys the best of Scotland's meat reared on the farms in the Scottish Highlands. Stuart also only uses wild venison from the clean environment of the rugged Scottish mountains. The traditional maturing process ensures that when the meat reaches the plate the taste and tenderness are the best possible. Stuart's free range pork from the Nairnshire coast is the best we have ever tasted.

www.stuartgrant.co.uk

Stuart Grant, Unit 6 Strathspey Industrial Estate, Grantown-On-Spey, Morayshire, Scotland, PH26 3JY.

Tel: + 44 (0) 1479 873 900

Ballindalloch Aberdeen Angus Beef from Millers of Speyside

Ballindalloch, situated on the banks of the Rivers Spey and Avon is a short drive from the premises of Millers of Speyside in the heart of the Scottish Highlands. The region is the historical home of the Aberdeen Angus breed, having been developed at Ballindalloch Castle during the 1800's by the local laird, Sir George Macpherson-Grant, 2nd Baronet of Ballindalloch. This herd is still in existence, is made up entirely of pure bred Aberdeen Angus, and is now one of the oldest cattle herds in the world. The meat is well marbled and matured on the bone for between 21 and 28 days.

www.millersofspeyside.co.uk

Millers of Speyside, Strathspey Industrial Estate, Grantown on Spey, Morayshire, Scotland, PH26 3NB.

Tel: + 44 (0) 1479 872 520

Demlane Mussels from Isle of Shuna Plc

Isle of Shuna is one of the largest independent producers of rope-grown Scottish mussels, both on the Scottish West Coast and the Shetland Islands which is where they produce Demlane mussels. Demlane is a well established brand which has built a reputation for superb quality and service. The cool, clear waters of the Shetland Islands, located off the North of Scotland coastline in the flow of the North Atlantic Drift, creates a favourable location which provides ideal growing conditions and an abundant food supply for these rope-grown shellfish. We only serve Demlane mussels in our restaurant as they have consistently proved to be of the best quality and taste, most easily cleaned and totally free from any grit.

www.isleofshuna.com

Isle of Shuna Plc, Walls, Shetland, Scotland, ZE2 9PF.

Tel: +44 (0) 1595 809348

Seafood from Andy Race

Based in the port of Mallaig in the Highlands of Scotland, Andy Race Fish Merchants is renowned for producing the very best Scottish peat smoked salmon, including organic smoked salmon, Mallaig kippers and a variety of high quality shellfish and smoked fish - all traditionally smoked with no resort to dyes.

www.andyrace.co.uk

Andy Race Fish Merchants Ltd. Mallaig, Inverness-shire, Scotland, PH41 4PX,

Tel: + 44 (0) 1687 462626

Meat and Speciality Foods from Buccluech Foods

With a tradition going back over 900 years, the finest quality Buccleuch beef is the first choice for many of the UK's premier chefs and restaurants and has graced the table of many state dinners. The full range of Buccleuch

produce; top quality cuts of the finest beef, lamb, pork and a delicious range of sausages, pies, sauces, conserves, mustards and desserts can be purchased on line.

www.buccleuchfoods.com

Buccleuch Heritage Brands, Station Yard, Oakwell Road, Castle Douglas, Scotland, DG7 1LA

Tel: + 44 (0) 1556 502 555

Arbroath Smokies from Iain Spink of Arbroath

With a history going back perhaps as far as the 15th century, Arbroath Smokies have been a staple of the east coast Scots. The hot smoked haddock can be eaten cold, hot or as an ingredient in soufflés, risottos in fact anywhere you want to use smoked fish. Iain's fish are smoked using traditional methods and are available at many farmer's markets and fishmongers throughout Scotland. Once eaten, never forgotten the golden flesh of the smokies is a truly mouth watering feast.

www.arbroathsmokies.net

Iain Spink, Forehills Farmhouse, Carmyllie, By Arbroath, Angus, Scotland, DD11 2RH

Tel: + 44 (0) 1241 860303

Miniature Bottles of Whisky from Just Miniatures

Most of our recipes use just less, or multiples of 50mls of the chosen whisky, it just so happens that this is the standard miniature bottle size. If you are having trouble sourcing the recommended whisky Just Miniatures will probably have it in stock.

www.justminiatures.co.uk

Just Miniatures Unit 7, Byford Court, Lady Lane Industrial Estate, Hadleigh, Suffolk, England, IP7 6RD

Tel: UK Free-phone 0800 634 8615
or +44 (0) 870 777 8017

Sourcing Ingredients for Recipes

Index

Index

Intellectual Property

The following names associated with ingredients in this cookbook are Registered Trademarks and Trading Names of:

Aberfeldy	Bacardi & Company Limited	Glengoyne	Ian Macleod Distillers Limited
Aberlour	Chivas Brothers Pernod Ricard Limited	Glenkinchie™	Diageo Scotland Limited
Ardbeg	Macdonald & Muir Limited	Glenlivet®	The Glenlivet Distillers Limited
Arran	Isle of Arran Distillers Ltd	Glenmorangie	Macdonald & Muir Limited
Auchentoshan®	Morrison Bowmore Distillers Limited	Hazelburn™	J. & A. Mitchell & Co. Limited
Balvenie®	William Grant & Sons Limited	Highland Park	Highland Distillers Limited
BenRiach	The Benriach Distillery Company Ltd	Jura™	Whyte and Mackay Limited
Benromach	Speymalt Whisky Distributors Limited	Knockando™	Diageo Scotland Limited
Black Bottle	Burn Stewart Distillers plc	Laphroaig®	Beam Global UK Limited
Bunnahabhain™	Burn Stewart Distillers plc	Longmorn	The Glenlivet Distillers Limited
Caol Ila™	Diageo Scotland Limited	Oban™	Diageo Scotland Limited
Cardhu	Diageo Scotland Limited	Old Pulteney™	Blairmhor Distillers Limited
Clynelish™	Diageo Scotland Limited	Royal Lochnagar	Diageo Scotland Limited
Columba Cream Liqueur	The Scottish Liqueur Centre Limited	Springbank	J. & A. Mitchell & Co. Limited
Cragganmore™	Diageo Scotland Limited	Talisker™	Diageo Scotland Limited
Dalmore™	Whyte and Mackay Limited	Teacher's®	Beam Global UK Limited
Dalwhinnie™	Diageo Scotland Limited	The Famous Grouse	Highland Distillers Limited
Drambuie®	The Drambuie Liqueur Company Limited	The Macallan®	The Macallan Distillers Limited
Edradour	Edradour Distillery Company Limited	Tomatin	The Tomatin Distillery Company Limited
Glayva™	Whyte and Mackay Limited	Tomintoul	Angus Dundee Distillers Plc
Glen Moray	Macdonald & Muir Limited	Tullibardine™	Tullibardine Limited
Glenfarclas™	J. & G. Grant		
Glenfiddich®	William Grant & Sons Limited	All information correct at time of publication	

Conversion Tables

As recommended conversions are never based on exact measurements you must never mix metric and imperial measures in the same recipe

Oven Temperatures		
°C	°F	Gas Mark
110	225	$^1/_4$
130	250	$^1/_2$
140	275	1
150	300	2
170	325	3
180	350	4
190	375	5
200	400	6
220	425	7
230	450	8
240	475	9

Spoon Measurements	
1 teaspoon	5 mls
1 dessert spoon	15 mls
1 tablespoon	20mls

Liquid Measure Conversion			
Imperial	Exact Conversion	Recommended Ml	US Equivalent
2.5 fl oz	71 ml	70 ml	$^1/_4$ cup
5 fl oz	142 ml	140 ml	$^1/_2$ cup
7.5 fl oz	214 ml	210 ml	$^3/_4$ cup
10 fl oz	284 ml	300 ml	1 cup
$^1/_4$ pint	142 ml	150 ml	0.3 pints (US)
$^1/_2$ pint	284 ml	300 ml	0.6 pints (US)
1 pint	568 ml	600 ml	1.2 pints (US)
$1^1/_2$ pints	851 ml	900 ml	1.8 pints (US)
$1^3/_4$ pints	992 ml	1 litre	2.1 pints (US)

Solid Measure Conversion		
Imperial/US	Exact Conversion	Recommended G
1 oz	28.35 g	25 g
2 oz	56.7 g	50 g
4 oz	113.4 g	100 g
8oz	226.8 g	225 g
12 oz	340.2 g	350 g
14 oz	397 g	400 g
16 oz 1 lb	453.6 g	450 g
2.2 lb	1 kilogram	1 kg